To

MYSTERIOUS MOMENTS

In the Paranormal

Best Wishes

Lillian

LILLIAN TYMCHUK

ξ DEDICATION ξ

In loving memory

of

STEVE and FLORENCE TYMCHUK

and

to all others who are aware of

and open to

the magic and mystery of life,

both visible and invisible.

PROLOGUE:

These stories are true.

Many are brief, merely faint fragments of time.

For the most part, people with whom I spoke thrilled with the excitement of having had a spontaneous, extraordinary and meaningful experience in their lives, one that left them with a feeling of surprise and astonishment, and usually with more questions than answers. Some felt that their own awareness and acceptance had allowed another dimension of reality to present itself. Still others did not appreciate the unasked for, unwanted, and poorly understood intrusion into their daily lives.

The concepts of space and time, normally considered to be constants, are thrown out the window in paranormal experiences as, for example, in the case of pre-cognitive dreams. Another example is in mental telepathy. As a point of interest, the electroencephalograph (EEG) was invented by German psychiatrist Hans Berger in 1929, to see if telepathy could be explained by brain waves.[i] Earlier, when Berger had been seriously injured, his sister strongly felt that something was wrong and convinced their father to send him a telegram. This impacted him to the extent that he switched his studies from astronomy to psychology.

What kinds of psychic phenomena are there? Precognition is the receiving of information about future events, whether in dreams or by a feeling, often a foreboding one. Telepathy is information exchanged between two minds. Clairvoyance is information received from a distance and is now known by the popular term "remote viewing." ESP refers to information received via any of the three previous means. Psychokinesis is mental interaction with animate or inanimate matter and is also called PK or telekinesis. Finally, the all-inclusive term is usually called psi.

Humankind has been experiencing the unexplained for eons, although serious research into the subject is relatively recent. In the 1970's, world-famous psychic Uri Geller familiarized the North American public with the paranormal using his uncanny ability to bend spoons. He currently is collaborating on the *Staya Erusa* film series which deal with quantum physics and the convergence of science and consciousness.

Dr. J.B. Rhine, called the "Father of Modern Parapsychology", performed his psychic experiments at Duke University in North Carolina. He became famous for working with the five symbols on the Zener Cards and for coining the term "extra-sensory perception" or ESP.

The 1973 Nobel prize winner of physics, Dr. Brian Josephson, is a staunch advocate of the possibility of the existence of paranormal phenomena and is director of the Mind-Matter Unification Project at the Cavendish Laboratory in Cambridge.

Dr. Edgar Mitchell, lunar module pilot of Apollo 14 and 6th man to walk on the moon, founded the Institute of Noetic Sciences and states that he himself was distance-healed of kidney cancer by Adam Dreamhealer, a young healer from western Canada. I had the honour of meeting Dr. Mitchell recently in Toronto.

The work of Dr. Michael Persinger, of Laurentian University in Sudbury, Canada, demonstrates that subjects can experience altered states of consciousness which in turn lead to mystical experiences. This is accomplished by the wearing of special helmets with low-intensity electro magnetic waves.

Dr. Dean Radin has investigated the concept of "entanglement" which suggests that on closer investigation, objects -- even solid ones -- aren't as separate as they seem and therefore can relate to each other throughout space and time.

Investigative journalist Lynne McTaggart, along with a host of physicists and other scientists around the world, is conducting web-based experiments to test the power of intention in changing the physical world, i.e. in testing the power of our thoughts. It would appear that the way to hell is not, in fact, paved by good intentions.

The purpose of this limited list is to indicate that serious interest and research are continuing into the study of the paranormal and the unexplained.

One of the first principles of research is the ability to replicate experiments at will. Here however, you will read about ordinary, day-to-day events with a twist, stories that have been accepted sans further research or the necessity for replication. The first chapter involves what seems to be trickery of the senses. Actually, *all* of the stories which follow may well be called *multi-sensory*, i.e. expanded beyond the limitation of the five senses.

Who has not tried to decipher one of their dreams or wondered about ghosts? Not surprisingly, children, healers and animals are more aware of, and more open to, the magical and the mysterious in life which, for them, are simply accepted as "normal." As for myself, I have long been awed by astounding stories of ships sailing on the seas, stories as wondrous as they are inexplicable.

Purely as an aside, the song *"Scarlet Ribbons"* has always fascinated me. The words are said to have "flowed onto paper" in fifteen minutes for lyricist Jack Segal in 1949 while visiting the home of concert pianist Evelyn Danzig Levine. Was this based on someone's real experience? Or, like the music of Mozart, was this beautiful song divinely inspired? I don't know -- but the lyrics are truly exquisite.

Skepticism, along with an open mind, is to be admired. However, I'm sure many skeptics will persist in saying that none of these true stories could have happened and that this is all a lot of nonsense anyhow, since they pitifully lack the ability to address the *possibility* of something viable beyond what has been taught, what is easily seen, and the ho-hum mundane. As a result, I feel I would be remiss if I did not address their worried little finger-tapping, white-knuckled rapping concerns. For them, the following information from *"Zen...and the Art of Debunkery"*© by Daniel Drasin should be most helpful in continuing their embedded, immoveable and unquestioning positions:

- *Put on the right face. Cultivate a condescending air that suggests that your personal opinions are backed by the full faith and credit of God. Employ vague, subjective, dismissive terms such as "ridiculous" or "trivial" in a manner that suggests they have the full force of scientific authority.*[ii]

Then there's always Lewis Carroll's approach in *Through the Looking Glass:*

Alice: "One can't believe impossible things."

"I daresay you haven't had much practice," said the Queen. "When I was your age, I always did it for half-an-hour a day. Why, sometimes I've believed as many as six impossible things before breakfast."[iii]

In conclusion, I would like to thank all who were kind enough to share their *different* experiences and those who helped in countless other ways.

Many people are gratified by the bounteous blessings that life has to offer, yet those who have been brushed by the mysterious are uniquely gifted with their glimpse – albeit brief – into the baffling and the unseen.

Lillian Tymchuk

April, 2008

CONTENTS:

Pictures:

ξ CHAPTER ONE ξ
SUBTLE SENSES

Ring out ye crystal spheres,
Once bless our human ears
(If ye have power to touch our senses so)
John Milton (1608-1674)

Each of us becomes accustomed to functioning in our own private world as best we can, using what we have been given. Our five senses -- seeing, smelling, touching, tasting, and hearing -- keep our inner world in touch with the outer world. We consider ourselves blessed when each of these functions performs perfectly without specific thought on our parts.

Most of us are aware that when someone lacks a specific sense, another sense may become more developed, such as improved hearing in the presence of blindness, or a perceptive sense of touch may help compensate through the use of Braille.

Not all is well-understood though. How do vision-impaired artists create beautiful paintings? And what about the times when the clearly visible becomes invisible, right in front of an entire crowd!

The term "second sight" or clairvoyance refers to the apparent ability to perceive future or distant events. "Sixth sense" on the other hand, is defined as "a supposed intuitive faculty giving awareness not explicable in terms of normal perception."[iv] *Perhaps such abilities do in fact exist, considering that we have terms to describe them.*

Then there is the purposeful blanking out of one sense to enhance another. An example can be found in the restaurants in which the 90-minute meals are eaten in total darkness, purportedly to enhance the taste sensations.

The sense of smell is the most primitive of the senses and always evokes memories. But what happens when someone smells flowers when none are there and this only occurs when a death in the family is imminent? Are natural laws at work in these instances? Or are they deemed unnatural until a rational explanation can be found?

At the Princeton Engineering Anomalies Research labs, (PEAR), scientists experimented with the effect of human intent on machines called random event generators or REGs. Interestingly, five REG computers showed enormous peaks when the verdict in the O.J. Simpson trial was announced on Oct. 3/1995, coinciding directly with the intense interest of some half-billion television viewers.[v]

Carrying on in the same vein, is there any way that machines can communicate with other machines, without any input from human beings? Apparently so, as you'll see shortly.

HIDING IN PLAIN VIEW

We were preparing for a huge graduation ceremony at the Royal Roads Military College in Victoria. Absolutely everything had to attain the peak of perfection for the Governor General, the plethora of VIPs, and the expectant crowd of some 5,000 - 6,000 tourists. We had worked extremely hard and were well satisfied that we had reached our goal of perfection.

Suddenly the Vice-Commandant's wife whispered to me in horror, "Annette, the Governor General's flag is upside down!"

This flag was positioned in the middle of the dais at the front of the parade square in full view of the entire populace. Such an incredible insult had to be corrected immediately.

I remembered watching *Kung Fu* and that Cane always said, *"If you believe they can't see you, they won't!"* These words raced around in my head, and suddenly I heard myself reassuring the Vice-Commandant's wife. "Don't worry, I'll fix it."

Now, I'm fairly tall and I was wearing heels. I was in full dress uniform. I left my chair, I walked down the seven steps, I strode out to the dais in full view of thousands of people, I marched up to the flag, I pulled the flag down the flagpole, I turned the flag around, I hauled it back up, and I walked back to my seat.

When the Vice-Commandant's wife looked at the flag again, she looked at me, puzzled. "How did you do that?" she said. "I didn't even see you."

And no one else did either. All the media was there and normally something like that would make front-page news. But the whole time I was out there, I was thinking, *No one can see me! No one will notice me!*

I was totally focussed inside my head on not being seen. My breathing was tightly controlled and I concentrated on not humiliating my boss. It was an extraordinary situation by any standard.

Nobody made any comment except the Vice-Commandant's wife. This was truly bizarre and I still keep joking about it. I say to my friends, "It's true, if I think I'm not here and that you can't see me, you can't!"

They all think I'm crazy, but I'm not. At Fort Bragg, the U.S. army base, some soldiers were actually being trained to do what I already did, i.e. make a person invisible. They were using techniques from ancient Buddhist monastic orders. Also, by concentrating on the fact that most solid objects like walls, desks etc. are actually made up of empty space between atomic particles, it was believed possible to walk through walls.[vi] Now, I haven't tried that yet, but I wouldn't be surprised if someone will able to do that successfully at some point.

Over the years people have asked me if I believe in reincarnation and I've always given the backhand answer, "Well I'm not sure I don't!" I have had déjà vu feelings that are really bizarre, in two different locations. There may be an explanation for the first one but definitely none for the second.

I find that whenever I'm in Quebec, I feel particularly comfortable and at ease, although I live in Ontario. I feel especially at home in the roadside taverns i.e. *les brasseries*, and I love French folk music. My father was raised in Montreal so I can't determine if my feelings are a product of his earlier conversations or not. I had been to France as a child for a short time as well but that didn't satisfactorily explain my feelings.

In 1985 I was in St. Jean, Quebec taking a course when we went into old Montreal for the evening. The restaurant we were in was extremely hot and uncomfortable so I went outside for some fresh air. As I wandered down the old cobblestone streets, I had to fight with myself because I wanted to enter the houses. I knew that I was acquainted with the people who lived there and was familiar with their homes, especially two or three in particular that I was aware had once been a part of me. The feeling was so intense that it scared me and I wondered what was happening. I've been back and forth through Montreal many, many times since and each time I've had that same *familiar* feeling.

I was in the military for twenty-five years and consequently travelled quite a bit. While on a military ship in Aarhus, Denmark, I recognized a déjà vu sensation similar to the one I always got in old Montreal. We were in Aarhus only for a couple of days but when the time came to leave, it was a real struggle for me because I didn't want to leave. It felt so much like home even though I had never before been there in my life. Not in this lifetime anyway...

With a little more nerve and a lot more money, I would have stayed there because it felt right, like home. I felt like I belonged there, like I had been there before. That was creepy because I didn't understand where my feelings could possibly be coming from.

Put me in France or Quebec and I'm laughing because at least I speak French but I certainly don't speak Danish. It all sounded so strange that I tried to deny my feelings because they made me nervous.

Now I sit back and think about all these things every once in awhile and wonder if I'll ever figure it all out.

A BLESSING AND A CURSE

Strange things used to happen in our farmhouse when we were growing up. The house had been built about eighty years prior, long enough for a couple of generations to make a home within its tidy red bricks.

For one thing, I never felt comfortable near Grandma's closet. After she died, I refused to sleep in her bedroom because I often *sensed* people around when no one was visible. None of my brothers, sisters, or cousins had this problem.

I was sixteen the first time something psychic happened to me in a big way. I woke up one hot summer morning and I could hear my dad saying, "Move the bales, the barn's overheating!" It was as if he was standing under my bedroom window. I jumped out of bed and looked out. My dad and brother were out at the back of the field with everyone else, bringing in the hay. I thought nothing of it and went back to bed. At noon that day, all the barns burned down!

Years later, after I married, my husband and I and our two kids, eight-year-old Madeline and six-month-old Brian, moved to a new home. That's when the strange occurrences escalated dramatically.

My parents had been to visit for the weekend and after they left, I was picking toys up from the living room rug. As I reached for a white dinky toy, it suddenly transformed itself into a full-size white car that roared across the living room, heading straight for me! Instinctively I jumped out of the way and then, just as suddenly, the car disappeared. I couldn't believe it! A full-size car in my living room? In Technicolour? The next day, a block away from our home, a full-size white car totalled the car I was driving and I suffered a severe whiplash. Time to pay attention.

As my young son got a bit older, I thought he must have inherited a psychic awareness because of little things that happened with him. He always seemed to be two steps ahead of us and he was very intuitive.

As the years passed, I started having recurrent dreams over a six-month period, dreams that I didn't understand despite their consistency. There was always someone on a bicycle and also the red tail-lights of a car. I didn't know who was riding the bike because I couldn't see the face and I certainly didn't know whose car it was.

I thought the dream might be a premonition and that I'd better be careful, that there might be someone on a bike who was going to pull out in front of me. The feelings were intense and dreadfully unnerving. As a result, I became afraid to drive.

This dream was a full-colour, movie kind of dream, but one where I was not really asleep. The sequence was this: turn out the lights, put my head on the pillow, and there it was. The bicycle followed by the red tail-lights.

One night there was a change. The face turned around and looked directly at me. I still didn't know who it was but I was extremely shocked.

The next day I got a phone call telling me that my seven-year-old son had been hit by a car while riding his bike, although the driver had slammed on his brakes. Brian died of his injuries.

When I returned home from the hospital after the accident, I lay down on the couch. I felt perturbed and uneasy. The house itself seemed unsettled in some way. The strange thing was that whenever I glanced at Brian's picture, it appeared to be three-dimensional.

Shortly afterwards, on Boy Scout Apple Day, one of Brian's friends brought some apples to the front door, which happened to be lined up with Brian's picture. The little boy took one look at the picture, shrieked, dropped his apples, and tore off down the street. Later he told us that it looked like Brian's picture was alive and that he was scared to death. That was enough. We took the picture down and put it away.

Soon it became obvious that there was something in our house, perhaps a resident poltergeist or a playful ghost. One day I swept the floor and put the broom back in the corner. It fell down. I picked it up, put it back in the corner, and down it fell again. This happened four times and my daughter and I simply stood staring at it. This was within a couple of weeks of Brian's funeral.

A lot of things disappeared. I would know exactly where I put something, go to get it, and find that it was gone. It got to a point where I'd say, "Listen you! Bring that back. I need it!" Later on I'd go back and the object would faithfully be where it should have been. This was not exactly something I felt I could discuss with my family doctor.

Four months after Brian's funeral, my brother and his wife came for an overnight visit with their two young boys. Early the next morning, my sister-in-law was sitting at the kitchen table with the kids. All of a sudden, her one little guy jumped off the chair and started running full tilt through the house. He returned to the kitchen all out of breath and said, "Who's that boy and why is he running so fast?"

It was pretty scary at first because we didn't understand this new and uncomfortable feeling. It seemed that I was always the first one to sense anything different, but generally I would keep it to myself and not say anything until somebody else did, usually my daughter. I never actually *saw* my deceased son, but my daughter told me she did and she was extremely upset by these encounters.

My husband didn't experience anything and oddly enough, he felt he missed something. He would have liked the experience of having further contact with his son. Altogether, it took seven or eight years for most of the eerie stuff to stop. I kept talking to my deceased son. Some friends who had been through a similar situation suggested this approach and it proved to be effective in the long run.

"It's okay, Brian," I'd say. "When you're old enough to go on, you can go. When you're ready to leave, you can leave."

At that point, I didn't understand what was happening in the world of the supernatural, but I knew I had to learn how to pay attention to the dreams that were going on in my head.

I think my dad could have been psychic too, but he might not have recognized it because he was in the age group that suppressed such experiences. One night I woke up and there was an older, rounded man with glasses standing in my bedroom. He was three-dimensional, solid, and full size, and appeared to be standing on the floor. He was looking straight at the bed. At that point, my dad had been diagnosed with cancer and he wasn't round anymore as he had become pretty thin, but it was the persona that we knew. I blinked and he was still there. This was about a month before my dad died and I thought he could have been checking in with me. He worried about me because I'm further away than the rest of the family.

"It's okay Dad," I said, "we're fine." I blinked my eyes again and when I opened them he was gone. I was amazed I could say anything to him at all.

Other things have happened since. One night my sister called to tell me that one of my brothers-in-law had been in an accident.

"Before you tell me what happened," I said, "let me tell you what I saw."

I told her about my dream which was like a black-and-white movie. There were three cars going in slow motion, and when two cars started to slide around, the third one ran off the road to dodge them. I gave her the exact location of the incident.

It turned out that's exactly what had happened. My brother-in-law's car wound up in the ditch to avoid hitting two cars that had skidded on the ice.

Shortly after that, I opened the door of the store where I was working and had to hustle out of the way because a car came barrelling through. After I moved over, I went outside and thought *did I just see a car or is that stupid?* The next day my husband's car was forced off the road on the mountain brow.

I had to learn how to put these things in their place, into some kind of perspective. There were two things that meant something was going to happen to someone in my immediate family. One was if my dreams, either in the sleeping or waking state, were in colour. The second was if something happened right there on the spot, like making me move to avoid being hit by a car. However, when I have a black-and-white dream, someone I know will be involved, but not my immediate family.

I'm not afraid of these dreams/movies and I don't spend a lot of time analyzing them. But if I see someone in a dream that I recognize, I might pick up the phone the next day and say, "How are you? What are you doing today?"

Sometimes what I see is like travelling the route beforehand. I called my sister one time because I was concerned about her and her family being on the highway to Toronto that weekend.

"Okay," she said, "tell me everything you saw in the dream, the whole pattern."

I told her I had seen some traffic congestion, red flashing lights, and some bales of straw.

After they got to Toronto, she called and said, "That's exactly what we encountered."

I either have dreams or wide-awake experiences. Sometimes there are uncomfortable feelings in our house where it doesn't feel *settled* or there are noises. That usually happens about forty-eight hours before I get a phone call that there's been an accident or somebody has died.

I also encountered a ghost at Stephen Leacock's house in Orillia. The tour guide provided a fascinating discussion as we ambled through each room. I love books, and of course I got waylaid in a library that was stacked with antique books. Since the tour group had already gone ahead, I thought I'd better hurry and catch up because I didn't want to miss the talks.

I walked up the stairs and saw the group on the left side of the hall. Since there was only one room on the right, I quickly went through the open door. Ouch! It felt like walking through an electric fence. There was nothing to see but I didn't know how I was going to get back out.

For once, I was really afraid. There was definitely something there. That *thing*, whatever it was, wasn't going to let me out and besides, I wasn't sure I wanted the experience of walking through the *electric fence* again.

I finally got up enough nerve to run out of the room and down the hall where I waited for the rest of the group. When they appeared, somebody opened one of the closet doors and said jokingly, "Is there a ghost in here?"

The tour guide said, "Well yes, as a matter of fact there is, but we don't talk about it much."

"The gh...gh...ghost is down the hall!" I stammered. They just looked at me.

The guide told us stories of how the ghost usually moved around in the middle of the night and turned off the alarms. She said the general consensus was that the spectre was Stephen Leacock's son playing tricks.

My latest movie was as recent as last night. In a typical black-and-white format, I could see three people in front of a window and others just milling around. One of my sisters has just flown out to British Columbia with her husband and five kids. I think what I saw was what three of the kids must have seen while looking out the airplane window.

I've never done a lot of reading on this topic but I did talk to some people after Brian's accident, for my own sanity. When I pieced things together, I realized these dream/movie sequences were meant to be warnings.

POSITIVELY GLOWING

My family is Catholic, and of course as kids we had to go to church every Sunday. Typically, I didn't like that idea, so I had to entertain myself somehow. I noticed that if I sat and stared at the priest, and focused directly on him, within a really short period of time a white glow would develop around his whole body. This always felt comfortable and soothing to me.

Many years later, as an adult, I was stationed on Ellesmere Island with the Canadian Forces for six months. We used to go out to Quiet Lake during daylight hours when we were allowed to leave the station. There were no sounds of any kind there. It's actually the first time I've ever heard total silence. There's no vegetation for the wind to make noise in and as I sat and stared, I would get a sense of a grey and cold-looking aura because the surroundings were so bleak and isolated. People who lived there tended to be lonely and very unhappy and I always wondered if that was why.

Here at home, I love to get up at 5:30 A.M. in the beautiful summer mornings, sit outside and stare at the trees and flowers. I get a peaceful feeling looking at plants that look like they are perfect and I almost feel like I'm watching from above. That's when I see a glow like the one that surrounded the priests of my youth.

I recently read *The Celestine Prophesy* and one of the principles that remained with me is that if you exude positive energy, other people can pick up on this force. Shortly after, I had an experience that illustrated this concept.

Every day I walked the same route to work in Trenton, passed the same groups of people, and always got the same quiet hellos in response to my "Good morning." Every once in a while I'd have a conversation with one of them.

I decided to test the principle of positive energy. Every day upon awakening, I would tell myself all of the great things about my life so that I felt extremely good and upbeat. This was surprisingly hard work but I got to the point where I felt really happy and I'd be bouncing along. Soon I was hearing "Hello, how are you?" and all of these people had broad smiles on their faces. I was amazed.

In fact, I was really astounded because it seemed that the happier I got, the happier was the response *to me.* And I wasn't yelling at them or doing anything different, I just gave them my usual "Good morning," but I was getting this amazing *"Good Morning!"* back from all of them.

The first few times it happened, I shook my head and looked at them. What's happening here, I wondered. I even looked behind me, looking for someone else they might be addressing, but there was no one else around.

Then I got lazy and stopped working on my own positive feelings and the response to me eventually decreased to the original lacklustre one. The effort I put into my state of mind, or lack thereof, corresponded perfectly with the responses I received. Until then I had never realized how much energy it took to be happy.

This weekend I'm trying another experiment. I've got some pretty stressed-out people to deal with, so I plan to work very hard at being happy myself and we'll see if my attitude will have any positive effects on them.

So this morning I said to myself, "All right, sweetie, you have to be really optimistic. You've got to feel really good inside and make it *look* as if you feel absolutely great too. These people must feel terrific when they're looking at you as opposed to everybody being tense. Because it seems you're the only one who is not super-hyper yet."

PUSH AND PULL

I had always been interested in psychic phenomena, especially out-of-body experiences (OBEs). But no matter how hard I tried, I was never able to accomplish an OBE. That is, until one night when I was in my late thirties.

I was having the experience of being in a hypnagogic state, half-awake and half asleep, when I realized that I was coming out of my body. My eyes opened but they weren't my physical eyes, they were my psychic eyes. I saw that while my body was firmly on my bed, my hands and feet were floating above the bed. Eerie as this was, I could see my limbs outlined in a greyish, luminous light.

Oh, I thought, *I'm coming out of my body. That's great! Then I'll come right out*!

Suddenly, my psychic sight flew to one corner of the bedroom and there, floating in the air, was a hooded figure. I never saw a face but I *knew* that this thing, whatever it was, was *pure evil.*

Scared out of my wits, I wanted to return to my body immediately! Kerplunkk! Down came the limbs and I was back in my bed. I woke up absolutely terrified because I knew without a shadow of a doubt that the greyish hooded figure was a malignant being. I felt confused and confounded as to what it may have meant, but thankfully long periods of time went by before I had another strange experience.

In the last three or four years however, I have noticed that when I've done a lot of extra work, am extremely physically tired, and feel absolutely depleted of energy, I seem to get onto a plane where other entities are able to attack me. There may be a sensation of a weight on the bed, or the feeling that somebody is sitting there or approaching me.

When I first go to bed, I go into quite a deep sleep that is actually the best sleep of the whole night for me. My husband usually comes to bed about half an hour after I do and his actions, like walking around the bedroom or going to the bathroom, wake me up.

It is in this time period when I'm half there and half not, that these *entities* as I call them, start pushing and shoving me and I can physically feel hands around my waist, squeezing.

Sometimes when I'm in a fetal position in bed, I can feel someone get in behind me, and tuck their knees in behind mine. This scares me half to death. I quickly push myself into full consciousness, cloak myself in a protective white light and say the Twenty-Third Psalm:

> *1 THE LORD is my shepherd: I shall not want*
> *2 He maketh me to lie down in green pastures:*
> *He leadeth me beside the still waters.*
> *3 He restoreth my soul: he leadeth me in the*
> *paths of righteousness for his name's sake.*
> *4 Yea, though I walk through the valley of the*
> *shadow of death, I will fear no evil:*
> *for thou art with me;*
> *thy rod and thy staff they comfort me.*
> *5 Thou preparest a table before me in the presence*
> *of mine enemies: thou anointest my head with oil;*
> *my cup runneth over.*
> *6 Surely goodness and mercy shall follow me all*
> *the days of my life: and I will dwell in the house of*
> *the LORD for ever.*[vii]

After I pray for protection, I close my eyes knowing that I am safe and go to sleep. That seems to do the trick.

The only explanation I can think of is that that while I'm in that semi-awake condition, I'm on an identical plane with these entities. I believe they are earth-bound people who haven't yet learned to move on. I'm so terrified that I'm not brave enough to let any kind of situation ever develop, but it seems to me if they were good entities they would leave me alone.

They seem to be attached to *me* rather than to a specific place, because this has happened to me in various places. When I was a youngster of twelve or thirteen, I fell asleep on the couch in the afternoon and had a similar experience. Then years and decades went by where nothing happened. This phenomenon frightens me because it's a very physical feeling.

When I tell my husband about it in the morning, he just laughs it off. He's a very well-grounded person. But when he was only fifteen, he had an interesting experience. At this time, he was apprenticed at work. One day, in the middle of his shift at the factory, at eleven o'clock, he had a sudden thought, *Granny just died.*

His grandmother lived with them and she had been sick, so it was quite logical that he should expect her death. But this particular thought, that she had gone, really appeared out of nowhere. When he got home, he asked his mother if Granny had died, and she said, "Yes, Granny died this morning at eleven."

That evening after he went to bed he saw the wraith of his grandmother float by his bed and disappear up the hall. It was just a goodbye and he wasn't the least bit scared. That was his one and only experience as opposed to all of mine.

PROPHETIC FRAGRANCES

I slowly slipped off my navy trench coat and the elegant black heels that I loved wearing. It had been a tiring day and I was glad to be home. Aunt Sophie had just come home from the hospital the day before after a severe heart attack and I had spent the entire day with her. There's weren't many other relatives left and the few remaining cousins, including Garrett and Marianne, lived too far north for me to spend much time with them. I wished Garrett lived closer as we had become good friends in college.

The drive to my aunt's little white frame house took about forty-five minutes on the back roads, but on a beautiful spring day when all the fragrant tulip trees were out, the drive was a treat in itself.

I had always been very fond of Aunt Sophie, my deceased mother's sister, and was saddened by her appearance in recent days -- the blue-ish tinge to her skin, the shortness of breath with the slightest exertion, and the chest pain when she even looked at the stairs. Aunt Sophie told me not to worry.

"This medicine always helps," said Aunt Sophie reaching for her nitro spray. "Now tell me about Pete, that handsome husband of yours. And your new job."

She had this knack of diverting the conversation away from herself and toward others. "So you're a bookkeeper now? How did you get to be so smart?"

As the day progressed I made myself useful, first in the kitchen and then just laughing and talking with my aunt.

When it was time to leave I said, "Now you call me if you need anything, Auntie. I'll give you a shout tomorrow night after work."

"Don't worry about me, dearie. The homemaker lady is coming. The VON nurse lady is coming. Everybody is coming. After being in that hospital, all I want is some peace and quiet," she said smiling, but with a tired expression in her eyes.

In the next three weeks, Aunt Sophie got stronger and her normal colour returned. She didn't get quite so out of breath and the chest pain didn't occur as often.

One Saturday afternoon, Pete and I stopped in to see her. She was in her flower garden, pulling out the weeds from between the delicate narcissus and the bright red and yellow tulips.

"Hello!" she called out to us.

"You missed some weeds over there," said Pete teasing her.

"Where?" She followed his pointing index finger. Then she realized she'd been had.

"Oh you," she said reaching up to swat his broad shoulders. "Come in and tell me what you're up to." She leaned her shovel against the side of the house. "I'll make you some Darjeeling tea and there's some nice fresh honey cake."

"Oh Aunt Sophie, I'm so glad you're feeling better, but don't you think you're doing too much?"

"No such thing, dearie. No such thing!"

After we got back home Pete said, "Auntie looks a lot better than last time. She really is such a sweet old lady."

"Nothing keeps her down for very long." I laughed. "As long as she has her cup of Darjeeling tea."

I paused, sniffing the air. "What's that smell?" I walked further into the living room, puzzled. "What's that smell, Pete? Flowers? Like in a florist's?"

"I don't smell anything."

"I'm telling you Pete, there's a heavy scent of flowers, roses. You know, like in a florist or a funeral home, or something like that."

I looked at him questioningly but he shook his head. "I don't know what you're talking about," he said.

The following day I was doing the dinner dishes when the phone rang. The VON nurse informed me that Aunt Sophie had had another heart attack, this one fatal. I couldn't believe my ears.

The next day was a blur, what with calling relatives, picking out the coffin, and arranging for the priest and the celebratory meal in the church to follow the funeral. I dreaded the moment when I would see my beloved aunt lying in a coffin.

When Pete and I walked into the funeral home, I tugged on Pete's coat jacket. "That smell! It's the same smell from the other

AROMATIC RED ROSES

night. At home. Remember?"

"What?"

"You know," I whispered. "That smell of flowers!"

"Yeah?"

"It's that same smell. Here in the funeral home!"

As we walked up to the coffin, all of my fears evaporated. Aunt Sophie looked peaceful and serene. We knelt and said a prayer for her soul and prepared to greet the other guests.

The funeral was fitting for Aunt Sophie, simple and dignified. It was also an opportunity to get caught up with relatives too, especially Garrett and Marianne, whose little kids had stayed home with a baby-sitter. The lunch prepared by the women from the church was luscious by any standards.

As I savoured the aroma of the steaming coffee made from freshly ground coffee beans, I was reminded of the incident with the weird smell of flowers, first at home and then at the funeral home.

"You know Garrett," I said, "the strangest thing happened the day before Aunt Sophie died."

I told him what had happened. His clear blue eyes took a grave turn. "I'm not surprised," he said. "I believe that events cast shadows before they actually happen."

I smiled gratefully. In some ways, he understood me when no one else could.

The ensuing days and months passed quickly. Pete had an offer to transfer to Montreal with another computer company but he and I made a decision to stay where we were, happy with our home and our jobs. How much money does anyone need?

A mutt by the name of Comet was soon to change our lives. He captured our hearts instantly and we brought him home. He was part German shepherd, part Husky, and part Lab. More than one old shoe found new quarters under our prize rose bushes in the west garden. Nonetheless, the puppy quickly learned to guard the house and the grounds despite his constant playfulness. Within nine months he had grown "to the size of a big Mac truck," as Pete liked to tell our friends.

One bitterly cold day in early February, Pete and I finished shovelling our long driveway after a heavy snowfall. Surprisingly, it was a chore that both of us enjoyed, more so now that Comet loved running and jumping in the snow so much. Finally I shook the snowy paw marks off my hat and coat and went into the house.

What's that weird smell, I thought. Smells like flowers at the florist's or something. I put the kettle on for the Darjeeling tea I had become so fond of. Hmmm. Four-thirty. Just enough time to get caught up with the antics of Victor and Nicky on the *Young & Restless* while the cabbage rolls and chicken heated up for supper.

The next day an urgent call was put through to me at the office. It was Garrrett's wife, Marianne. She was sobbing as if her heart was broken.

"What's the matter?" I asked. "Slow down and tell me what's going on."

"It's Garrett," she cried. "He's dead."

"Garrett?" I asked incredulously. "Dead? What happened?"

"He was shovelling snow," she sobbed. "He had a heart attack. This morning."

I couldn't believe it. My favourite cousin was gone and only thirty-seven years old. My scattered thoughts raced to the scent of flowers yesterday. I thought of Garrett's words at Aunt Sophie's funeral.

Maybe events really do cast shadows before they occur.

Post Script: Does it scare me? No. Strangely enough, it goes out of my mind until after the next one happens. But it's always the same smell, like at a florist or a funeral home. And always the day before the death of someone I know.

ANOTHER "LEGEND"? ©

It is 28 October 1997. Yesterday morning I was trying to get down to my job as a writer, but it was Monday, I had spent a sedentary weekend, and I had a strong desire to golf. I like to play either alone or with people I know, but I decided to take a chance and just show up at the course, and if some stranger wished to join me, so be it. As usual, I arrived at an unusual time - "unusual" in that not many golfers appear at 11:30 A.M. - so there would be a good chance the first tee would be free. Especially as it was late in the golf season, and a blustery day with low threatening clouds whipping across the sky. But on top of an undershirt and a long-sleeve sweater, I wore a short sleeve sweater and a light jacket.

Just a note about the golf course. Called "Camisle", it described itself as "The Land of Legend." It is an amazing place, with a central complex of rough-hewn, big-timbered buildings with a definite rustic look. Scattered over the course are large wooden sculpture-like structures, some serving as bridges over water hazards and there are numerous manmade earthen mounds, often with a standing stone atop. I was reminded of prehistoric sites I had visited in Britain, especially Stonehenge and its surroundings.

When I arrived there was just one other car in the parking lot and my heart leaped. I paid my green fees and went immediately to the first tee. The first hole is 170 yards over a large pond, but I hit a nice 7-wood, pin high just off the right edge of the green. Beside the green, in addition to my ball, there was another. Unlike almost all balls found on the golf course, this was in absolute plain view. I appeared to be the only one around, so I picked it up. It was brand new, and absolutely glistened in its pristine whiteness! I didn't recognize the brand name; it was definitely one I had never seen before, and I have played for many years. Most golfers have a particular brand they prefer, mine being Titleist. My find was a "logo ball", advertising a company. This logo was a rich green, scroll-shape, and, although I don't remember the name of the company printed on the scroll, it was something like "Wecom." At any rate, I had never heard of it.

I put the ball in my left jacket pocket, along with my spare Titleist. I played the first three holes pretty well - for me - getting a bogey on each. When I arrived at Number Four I was feeling euphoric; I was on my game, and there seemed to be nobody else on the nine-hole course. Or even on the eighteen-hole course which adjoined it. Amazing! I had it all to myself. Number Four is especially memorable for me. A few weeks before, my brother had visited and I took him along to Camisle. The Fourth is a difficult hole; 325 yards long, it was a wide fairway which gradually closes as it approached the green between stands of trees on each side, leaving only a narrow opening to the green. Twenty yards in front of the green is a small creek, but I didn't bother telling my brother as nobody ever comes close to it with their drive. My brother stepped up, took a mighty swipe, and drove his ball to the green! After he sank his ten-foot putt for an eagle (two under par) I told him it hadn't happened; that what he had done was impossible!

I hit a long drive, but it angled left into the trees. When I found it I realized I had what seemed like a straightforward nine-iron shot over some trees to the green. I was relishing hitting it, but I shanked it and it hopped left near a pond. I took another mighty swipe but almost missed and the ball skittered twelve feet, ending up behind a small tree. Stymied, I dubbed my next shot another dozen feet into a pond, where it sank forever.

I reached into my pocket for my spare Titleist and found that the other ball was missing. This was very odd, and I could only conclude it had fallen from my pocket when I bent to retrieve my ball from either the second or third hole. But in that case, how come I still had my Titleist? I felt a pang at the loss of the beautiful, unusual ball, but soldiered on.

By the time I left Number Four I had taken nine shots, seven more than my brother! Any chances of scoring well that day were over, so I would just have fun. I walked to the tee of Number Five, and hit a lovely 7-wood to the front of the green. I had hit it firmly and it had positively soared! Beautiful! I walked quickly up towards my ball but halfway there I spotted another, smack dab in the middle of the fairway. What luck! To find two like this during the same game! I picked it up and found it was identical to the ball I had found on the first hole! In fact, it could have been the same ball, as it was perfect. How odd! I put it in the left pocket of my jacket again and carried on.

I hooked my tee shot on Number Six into the woods, and listened as it rattled around, a golfer's worst sound! Thinking it might be lost I reached for my left pocket; my new ball was still there, but I suddenly had a feeling that it was somehow very special. I hated to soil it by hitting it, but thought there may be something magical about it - I might hit it a mile! I teed it up and swung away. I shanked it badly, even worse than the first shot, but I watched carefully to see where it dropped. I retrieved it and put it back in my left pocket.

There it stayed until I was just off the back of the green on Number Eight. My approach shot was too short, so I thought I would try it again with my new ball. What the hell, there still was nobody else on the course, so I wouldn't be holding anybody up. Normally it is crowded, so having it to myself was a seeming miracle. Also the weather really wasn't that bad, with a few healthy gusts now and then. My second approach was as pathetic as the first, so I picked up my new ball and put it back in its accustomed pocket. And there it stayed. On the Ninth Hole I found three balls, which helped console me for having taken an eight on both Number Eight and Number Nine.

I finished my round and, as there was still nobody else on the course, I went back and played the last two holes again. Then I emptied my pockets of all balls and tees into my golf bag, threw it in my car and drove home. When I got there I took my golf bag to the basement, and, just for fun, emptied my bag of golf balls to check them out. I had lost a few, but found a few; I now owned a Pinnacle, a ProStaff, a Top-Flite and a Fantom Gold. But speaking of

"Fantom", I suddenly realized there was one ball missing. The lovely glistening new one with the green logo. Again it had mysteriously disappeared. I had a sudden spook realization that somehow I was never meant to own it, because it had never really existed!

To sum up, I found the ball on the First Hole, discovered it was lost on the Fourth Hole, found it again on the Fifth Hole, and somehow lost it once more.

Explanations? An employee of "Wecom" - or whatever - was playing a round of golf, and had inadvertently left a pocket of his golf bag open, and balls fell out accidentally. Or perhaps he was the president of the company, and had so many of his "logo balls" that now and then he couldn't be bothered to pick one up. Maybe he thought it good advertising for some stranger to find one.

But I don't think so. I believe my story is now part of the lexicon of The Land of Legend.

Robert Nielsen, Publisher and Author

Stoney Creek, Ontario

SMOKE ALARM

"Make sure the battery in that smoke alarm is set!" my father would tell each of us. Actually it got to be a joke because every time he saw any of his three married children, he always said the same thing.

"Make sure the battery in that smoke alarm is set!"

He was a mechanic and really into safety features. Although we kidded him, we loved him all the more for his concern for our well-being.

This spring, unexpectedly, my father passed away peacefully in his sleep. About a week after he died, my daughter and son-in-law stopped by for dinner. Naturally, we talked about "Grampa." After they left, I was downstairs watching TV and my sixteen-year-old son was up in his room.

Suddenly the smoke alarm gave one unusually loud, long and piercing beep. I thought, oh great, the battery is going, and lay on the couch waiting for it to go off again. But it didn't.

My son was in his room on the third floor with the stereo blaring. He ran down the stairs to see what happened.

"What was that?" he asked, puzzled.

"The smoke alarm," I said.

Okay, at least I wasn't the only one who heard it. Later I tested the smoke alarm and there was absolutely nothing wrong with it. I really don't know why I bothered testing it. I knew all along that it was my father, and I felt comforted and reassured.

HAVE YOUR PEOPLE CALL MY PEOPLE

By the time I moved in with Allan, my boyfriend in New York, Rick and Dawn, the couple that were his best friends, had become my best friends too. We went to many concerts together, bonded by a love of deafening guitars, Mick Jagger, *suicide* chicken wings and draft beer.

Rick and Dawn lived in an old, old house that sat on a pretty piece of property in the country. Nonchalantly, they reported that their house was full of ghosts and that they had gotten quite used to them. The two of them would be reading in the kitchen and they'd hear a whole family laughing and chatting in the dining room. Rick and Dawn just laughed because they were used to weird things occurring there. Although they could never actually make out any of the ghostly conversations, Cobby, their growling little Scottish terrier wasn't exactly ecstatic about the extra occupants. A little research indicated that several large families had successively occupied the house after it was originally built.

Other times when Rick and Dawn might be relaxing on the wrap-around porch on a summer evening, the old tree swing would start swaying back and forth in a nice even rhythm at first and then swinging higher and higher until it would eventually slow down and stop, all by itself.

Their weirdest experience however, happened when they were in bed one night. They saw a young woman appear out of nowhere, dressed in old-fashioned garments from years gone by. Moments later, she disappeared as suddenly as she had appeared. They accepted this experience as part of the charm of their old house.

All of our schedules were extremely busy as we juggled university classes with full and part-time jobs and it got harder and harder to keep in touch. It seemed everybody was on a different schedule. Thankfully we had an answering machine, as did they. One week in October, we had tried to call them several times and ended up leaving short messages like, "Hey you guys, you haven't called!"

Then one day when my boyfriend and I both came home from work there was a message flashing. When we played it, we couldn't figure it out:

"Hi. You've reached Dawn & Rick. We're unable to take your call at the moment, but if you leave your name and number, we'll get back to you as soon as possible. See ya!"

Somehow their answering machine had called our answering machine and left their recorded message! When we finally got in touch with them a week later, they said, "Oh, we've been away on vacation."

At Christmas they went down south and once more the same thing happened. In fact, every time they went away, their answering machine would phone our answering machine. We called the phone company and there was no explanation. My explanation was that the ghosts got tired of hearing us say, "When are you going to return our call?"

This experience gives new meaning to the phrase "Have your people call my people." I figured it was pretty neat that those ghosts were keeping up with technology.

ξ CHAPTER TWO ξ

GHOSTS & OTHER GALACTIC GUESTS

Night's swift dragons cut the clouds full fast,

And yonder shines Aurora's harbinger;

At whose approach, ghosts, wandering here and there,

Troop home to churchyards.

William Shakespeare (1564 – 1616)

Ghosts, spectres, wraiths. What are they? Is it possible to communicate with them?

A ghost is defined as "an apparition of a dead person which is believed to appear or become manifest to the living, typically as a nebulous image," [viii] *while a spectre is associated with something unpleasant or dangerous. A wraith, (thanks to 16th century Scots for such a wonderful-sounding word) is a ghostlike image of someone seen shortly before or after their death and can present a way of saying goodbye to loved ones who are not physically present at the time of death, whether traumatic or non-traumatic.*

Where did the first ghosts stories appear? In the Bible! Perhaps one of the oldest written reports of a ghost story is in the first book of Samuel, chapter 28. Here Saul asks the medium of Endor to conjure up the deceased Samuel to help him. Samuel subsequently appears to Saul as an old man covered with a mantle i.e. a loose shawl or cloak. According to writer Brian Innes, this mantle incident may explain the predilection of our Western culture for sheet-covered ghosts.[ix]

Are there ghost stories in our current culture? The popular soap opera, "The Young and the Restless," is known for dealing with contemporary topics, such as the importance of knowing CPR for children. Recently the long-standing character of John Abbott, introduced in 1982, died and later re-appeared as a ghost. His son, Jack is the only one who can see and hear him.[x] *Abbott looks like he did in "real" life and has normal conversations with his son, often dispensing much-needed advice. While the ghost of Abbott appears and disappears at various times, he cannot be summoned up at will by his son. Numerous university courses dissect the impact of such topical programs on the viewing public and it is noteworthy that the writers have chosen this particular story line now.*

So much for ghosts. What of other inter-galactic guests? A well-known paranormal investigator shares the strange events that set him on the path of a fascinating career. And then a much-respected mystic transports you, dear reader, on an astonishing astral journey.

The men and women who share the following stories know at their deepest levels that these enticing encounters are totally authentic.

THINK ABOUT IT

When my parents split up, my dad took me to live with his mother. I lived with my grandma from the time I was two until I was five. By then all of her seventeen kids were grown up and gone and I was the only one of all her grandchildren that she looked after. This little hump-backed grandma of mine was a saint in my eyes. She was always there for me and I could talk to her about anything.

My grandparents were very wealthy and owned lots of property. I can remember the maid carrying me up and down the stairs early in the morning. But it wasn't always like this. My grandfather was an alcoholic and the only reason he wanted so many children was to have somebody to run the farm.

When I was almost six my dad brought me half way across the country to live with my aunt and uncle and then he went off to join the war effort. I never forgot my grandma and every Christmas I begged my aunt to send her flowers from me.

When I was eight, my aunt and uncle took me to visit Grandma once more and I was in seventh heaven. She hugged me so hard she took my breath away. Then, with a twinkle in her eye, she said, "Come with me. I want to show you something very special."

I followed her into the bedroom where she pulled open the middle drawer of her high dark dresser. There covered by white tissue paper, were all the Christmas flowers I had ever sent her. I was glowing enough to light a seven hundred watt light bulb.

She died when I was fifteen and I was totally devastated. I kept returning to look at the few pictures I had of her, as if to gather strength. As the years passed, I got married and was busy raising my own family, but I never forgot Grandma.

About five years ago one of my girlfriends told me that she had developed her psychic powers and could see auras. I didn't put much stock in that and told her so.

"I can see your aura and it's purple… but it's the weirdest thing.

"What's weird?"

"Every time I'm with you, I see this older person, kind of bent over, standing behind you."

I paled visibly.

"She's old and she's bent over," she continued.

"She's not bent over," I whispered. "She's got a humpback."

"Yes, that's it."

I hadn't even told my husband about my grandma, let alone anyone else, but my girlfriend described her perfectly. I told her about the special bond we shared. What I didn't tell her though, is that I have constantly talked to my grandmother because I felt that she was always there for me and still is.

When I'm really feeling down, I sit in a chair, close my eyes, and talk to Grandma out loud, not in my head. I can see her from the waist up. We have a regular conversation, one that I doubt anybody else could hear. If I'm extremely upset, she paces the floor with me.

If I present a problem to her she'll say, *Think about it.* She'll remind me not to be selfish and to *be mature*. These are the kinds of things I have come to expect from her.

When I've had a fight with someone and wish I had said this or that hurtful thing, Grandma says, *Well, maybe not saying those things is the right thing to do. Think about what you're doing. Do you want to hurt somebody? Think about why you're doing it. You're angry and you're hurt. But why are you hurt? Is it because you didn't get your own way or because you just want to hurt back? Maybe you deserved it.*

That's probably why I'm so calm now and never fly off the handle like I used to. She and I have had so many conversations. She's my conscience.

The last time I talked to my grandma was just before Christmas -- obviously my life has been pretty smooth. Even on a good day though, I still talk to her. She's my mentor. She's my reality check.

METAPHYSICAL MOTHER

When I'm ready to go to sleep, it's not uncommon for me to feel ghostly fingers playing with my hair. Or they may touch my arms and if I look, I can clearly see their imprint on my skin.

My mother, who has long since been deceased, still has a way of turning up periodically, especially if there is illness in our widespread family. My brother and sisters always say, "Mom will turn up forever. And she'll get you if you're not doing the right thing."

Recently one of my sisters said, "Good Lord, that old lady came and kept me up all night."

I can sense her presence and I feel comfortable when she's here. I talk to her non-stop. Verbally. Out loud. She doesn't answer per se but I do know when she arrives, that somebody may need a prayer.

Whenever my brother is ill, she comes to me and then I realize that oh, oh, Desmond must be in trouble. The last time she arrived, he had a heart attack and had to have a bypass.

My sister can see things. Desmond came home one time to Georgetown, Guyana and he was really ill with a very high fever. She had done all she could for him.

During the night she went to check on him and she saw my [deceased] mother there. My sister said, "Well I can't do anything else for Desmond. You can look after him, Momma."

Momma continued sitting there on Desmond's bed, stroking his head.

In the morning his fever had broken.

BURNING BRUSH

My dad was a tall, broad-shouldered man with a magnificent handlebar moustache, a strong Saskatchewan farmer who never seemed to be afraid of anybody or anything. But this one time even he was shaking with fear.

It all happened in the 1920s, when my dad had to go to Grandfather's farm to bring back some wheat. He hitched up a pair of matching horses that could withstand a heavy load and decided to take the shorter, rougher road while the wagon was still empty. Because Grandfather himself was putting seed in for his wheat field, Dad had to go when Grandfather would be through for the day and therefore have enough time to weigh out the amount he was selling to Dad for seed.

After supper, they measured out the proper amount of seed and it was just getting dark when Dad started out for home. This time he took the longer way on account of the heavy load of wheat seed. The horses were young, well fed, and frisky, given to cantering even when hitched up to a wagon. He trusted them completely. Once when he had become lost coming home in the dark from the mill, he gave them the reins and they brought him home safely, stopping at the gate and whinnying softly to be let into the barn.

But coming up the hill now with the seed covered by a tarpaulin, Dad could not figure out why they acted in such a strange manner. They seemed to want to get off the road and pushed close to each other as if they were frightened. As they came up on the hill, Dad saw a fire burning in a small brush and in it, standing, was a woman! The fire was all around her and yet she didn't appear to be burning.

By now the terrified horses were snorting and pushing so hard against the wagon tongue that Dad thought the neck-yoke would get broken. He was afraid that if the wagon slipped off the trail, he'd get stuck because of the heavy load. He was so petrified he tried to make the sign of the cross, but the reins had to be kept so tight that he couldn't. He prayed out loud, all the time grasping the reins so the horses would get through the road where the fire was burning.

Once the horses got past the fire, there was no stopping them. They cantered all the way home, snorting. My dad didn't know what to make of what he had seen or if he did, he wasn't saying. But clearly it wasn't an illusion as the horses had reacted to the burning brush and the woman as well.

We never found out who the woman was, but I know I have never seen my dad so scared either before or since.

MISSING RINGS

My grandmother passed away almost a year ago. I was very close to her and used to drive her back and forth to the hospital for her cancer treatments. She fought as hard as she knew how but the breast cancer ravaged her body and she deteriorated quickly. It tore my soul apart to see what was happening to her.

About two weeks before she died, she looked at me with a glint in her eye. For a moment or two she looked like the strong Grandma from my childhood.

"I want you to have my engagement and wedding rings and I want Stacey to have my mother's rings."

Stacey was my first cousin.

"Okay Grandma, thanks for telling me that, but I want you to be around for a lot longer."

When she died, her engagement and wedding rings were still on her finger. The funeral home director took them off and gave them to my uncle, Stacey's father. I was torn. I didn't know what to do. Finally I spoke to my dad.

"Dad, I don't want to say this, but it was Grandma's wish that I get her engagement ring and her wedding band. I don't know where the other rings are for Stacey, but I know I'm supposed to get her rings."

He spoke to my uncle who said that the rings Grandma had once belonged to Great-grandma and that they belonged to Stacey. There were no other rings as far as he knew. As a result, there were a lot of hurt feelings.

I didn't want to say, "Look they're mine!" because it didn't feel right to be fighting over something like that. But it kept gnawing at me because I knew Grandma wanted me to have them. And I knew there were two sets of rings because Grandma told me so.

One day I decided I needed some time to myself. I ended up going to Grandma's house and let myself in with my key. We had already gone through the whole house from top to bottom and removed all the valuables because the house would soon be empty and we were afraid someone might break in. But no one had found the missing rings.

It was upsetting because I didn't want this family bickering to be going on. Still, I knew what her wishes were and I hoped the other rings would be found.

I plunked myself down in Grandma's favourite pink plush chair in the living room and said, "Grandma, you know, things would be so much easier if you could've just told me where the rings were, or if you had shown me where you kept them. Things would work out much easier at this point. It's so trivial, but... it would be great."

I looked around at everything she loved. She had shelves filled with knickknacks, each one special in some way. After a few moments, I decided to leave. Just then a flash of light bounced off a little red vase on the shelf. No more than two inches high, the depression-glass vase was rimmed with gold.

"How bizarre," I thought. "What was that anyway?"

I took a closer look and saw there was something in the bottom of the vase. I turned it over and what fell into my hands but the very rings we had all been searching for. I couldn't think. I couldn't speak.

Finally I said, "I always knew you were around, Grandma. Thanks for showing me where the rings were."

NIGHTMARE IN WHITE ©

My wife and I and our three children lived for more than twenty years in a house in Westdale, a well-established neighbourhood in Hamilton. It was a medium-sized two-story house with a large attic. On the second floor there were three bedrooms, two in front and one in back.

We had lived in Westdale previously, then moved elsewhere for five years, and now were back in Hamilton. We wanted to live in Westdale again, but couldn't afford it. Nevertheless one day we were driving through, and noticed a house for sale. We made a viewing appointment and when we showed up, in addition to the real estate agent, there was a little old lady and her son or son-in-law. It turned out the family were eager to get her out and into a nursing home and they were ready to listen to an offer. Especially from us, apparently, as the old lady thought we were a nice young couple worthy of living in her house. We made a lowball offer, and to our astonishment it was accepted.

As to there being anything odd about the house, there was the fact that the living and dining rooms were papered with a heavy, expensive, deep gold wallpaper that made the place seem very gloomy. There was also the fact that Mrs. C., a previous resident, had passed away in a bedroom upstairs -- the day after her one-hundredth birthday.

I myself never experienced anything of a supernatural nature in the house -- that is, while I was awake. One night I had a vivid nightmare about going down to the basement, where an evil, skinny, hunch-backed, little white-haired man wearing a hideous grin was madly whitewashing the walls. He would tear up to me now and then, stare mockingly, and then rush off somewhere else in the basement to begin wildly painting again. I woke in a state of sweaty terror; I could literally feel my backbone shuddering from the horror of having met the ghost of someone connected to the house, a wicked, cunning and terribly keen presence. The next day I was speaking to my next-door neighbour. Although I said nothing about the dream, he asked me if I knew that the previous owner had died of a heart attack while painting the outside of the house.

My sister-in-law, who is really into such things, believed that the second floor of our house was haunted by an unpleasant woman. She hated to go upstairs to the bathroom on her own for this very fact. Hence, she was not surprised by the various experiences that other people had.

My wife shared my sister-in-law's belief, but being a brave, no-nonsense type, she claimed the lady was harmless -- but definitely a presence in the house. Normally a deep sleeper, one night she woke and looked out into the hall, where she saw a white fog, in the shape of a person. Fearing it might be smoke, she got up, went into the hall, and wafted a hand through it. It immediately dispersed. She believes -- adamantly -- that it was a ghost. On another occasion, in the back bedroom, one of my sons awakened to find a lady in "an old-fashioned dress" standing beside his bed. She didn't speak, and soon disappeared.

I turned the unfinished attic into a room which served as my other son's bedroom. He awoke one night to feel someone lying on top of him. But there was no physical presence. He asked quietly if the person would get off him, which happened immediately. Some years later, when my son had left home, I turned his bedroom into my office. But when company came it served again as a bedroom. My daughter-in-law was sleeping there one night and awoke to the same sensation. An invisible person was lying on top of her, but eventually left. Needless to say, both victims of the heavy-bodied spirit found the experience terrifying.

I experienced none of these phenomena, and never could bring myself to believe they were "supernatural." I didn't want to believe, as the thought of it was too frightening, and I had to live there! However, the people who did experience them are highly credible, and to be believed. Why did the "ghost" of the woman on the second floor never appear to me? I think that if there are such entities, they show themselves only to people who are empathetic, and who are able to sympathize with the plight of those who are, perhaps... gone, but not gone?

Robert Nielsen, publisher and author

Stoney Creek, Ontario.

THEATRICAL GHOSTS

Theatre Royal in Chatham, Kent (England) has for many years been famous for reports of strange noises and happenings from the present time going back to the 1st World War. The theatre was built on the site of an old brewery on High Street and opened in 1899 with a seating capacity of 3,000.

The most well known ghost at the theatre is Humphrey, who is regarded as its guardian through two World Wars, its closure, the town centre development, and threats from various property developers.

Humphrey is thought to either be the ghost of an artist who hung himself in the theatre, or else a member of the theatre staff who was responsible for counting the takings of both the *Theatre Royal* and *Barnard Theatre of Varieties.* The latter was opposite a music hall owned by the Barnard brothers, also proprietors of the *Theatre Royal.*

Former employees claimed Humphrey was a friendly if mischievous ghost who appeared on the stage, the dress circle, or in the upper balconies, commonly called "the gods," and walking through locked doors. The theatre's cleaners often opened doors for him in awe and respect to him!

He is credited with moving or losing objects. A former dancer at the theatre, Sylvia Flaherty, often saw him sitting in the dress circle watching performances. If he did not like what he saw, he would walk out and slam the door behind him.

In 1954, a newspaper article recorded the experiences of investigator Mr. Fred Sanders who spent the wee hours with Humphrey in the theatre auditorium. In the *Chatham Observer*, Joan Copley, a well-known local amateur actress, described how Humphrey sat and watched dress rehearsals.

In the same article, Mr. Sanders described other ghosts such as "Charlie," the ghost of Charlie Monks, a former employee. He also describes the sighting of a "Green ghost," the shining figure of a man who haunted one of the boxes and was also seen in the local department store next door.

Sanders found distinct differences amongst the three ghosts -- Humphrey could be sensed, Charlie could be heard, and the Green ghost could be seen. Sanders believed all three moved between the theatre and the former music hall site. Local people also reported inexplicable noises and occasional music in the building.

More recently, since the theatre was bought by the Theatre Royal Trust, volunteer workers have found tools being moved, electrical equipment turning off for no reason, and at least one sighting of a figure.

Psychic investigators visited the theatre looking for answers. During one session a tape recorder recorded a series of high-pitched musical notes in a descending scale, although strangely enough, none of those present heard these sounds. However they did feel like they were being touched by the ghosts. The investigators concluded that there may be a number of ghosts in the theatre.

One investigator thought he discovered the spirit of an old woman who died in the theatre in a lavatory in about 1911. There certainly were indications that the most haunted room in the theatre was the ladies' toilet in "the gods."

Recently local policemen used the room for a stakeout. They experienced chairs falling over, doors slamming, ghostly hands on their shoulders and other strange occurrences. Not surprisingly, they refused to return the next night. The same things happened to their replacements.

In the autumn of 1996, new ghosts made their presence known in the theatre auditorium. A strange scent of old-fashioned tobacco, there one moment and gone the next, was noticed by theatre volunteers. No smoking is allowed in the theatre and after hours of trying, no one could trace the origin of the smell.

While naturally there will be those who will be skeptical of such accounts, the frequency and nature of these stories do give the impression of something very special about the *Theatre Royal Chatham.* Certainly it would not be unreasonable to claim that it reputedly remains Britain's most haunted theatre.

Richard Parker, Chairman: Friends of the Theatre Royal England

ROYAL GHOSTS

Windsor Castle, where I work, is situated in Berkshire, England, a small town on the Thames River just west of London.

The county of Berkshire is rumoured to be one of the most haunted counties in all of England and today is well known for numerous hauntings and various ghosts. Bisham Abbey, training centre for England's football team, is frequented by the ghostly Lady Hoby who it seems, is destined to roam the corridors forever, after accidentally killing her son.

I was working there as Membership Secretary in a lovely old room with very high ceilings and beautiful alabaster motifs. I often had to look for files as we have thousands of members in our organization. The files were often inexplicably mixed up, although they were never completely missing.

One of the filing cabinets contains four drawers with the files arranged alphabetically. I might look for a particular file and it would not be there. I would discover that a little lump of files would have been moved from one section of a drawer perhaps two or three inches away to another section of the same drawer, but obviously they were no longer alphabetical. For instance, some of the "C" files would be in the "F" section. This happened behind closed, locked doors.

Several times, I knew I had placed a file in its proper alphabetical spot just before going home, locked the door, and when I returned the following morning, the file would be in a different spot, and I knew no one else had been in the room.

I just thought it fun, that the imps were playing. There didn't see to be a specific trigger for these occurrences. There was no explanation. We simply shrugged our shoulders and carried on.

On one occasion one of the secretaries had spent all day writing and typing letters. At the end of the day, she left the pile of letters on her desk to attend to the next morning. They were found all smothered in something black, and we couldn't ascertain whether it was smut, dust or just what it was. They certainly were quite unusable. The workmen looked everywhere through the ceiling to see where on earth it had all come from but they couldn't find out. She had to redo all the letters.

I'm not in that office now because we've moved and it only happened in one particular room. It's still used but not as the room we work in. It's more of a storeroom with filing cabinets and boxes of things to do with aspects of the office. We are in there daily but there's nothing for the imps to play about with that we would notice.

Now I'm in another room in the same building, in what was the caretaker's bedroom. Strangely, absolutely nothing happens there, which is odd to me because the building is terribly old. This room is the life of the building and has had a lot of people coming and going. Being here is jolly nice because we're on our own as it were, except that we share it with the stonemasons. They have what they call their little canteen in one of the rooms and in it is a sallyport or trapdoor built into the wooden floor. This leads to beautifully built steps that wind down to a brick tunnel that goes right through to the River Thames. It was built as an escape route for messengers in case of siege.

GHOSTS IN GUYANA

I have always felt thc presence of the unseen world, even when I was growing up in Guyana. My youngest sister actually saw "them," all manner of ghosts and spirits. Often in the middle of the night, she would jump on my bed and shake me by the shoulders.

"Inez, there's somebody sitting out there and I have to go to the bathroom!"

I couldn't see anybody but I *sensed* that someone invisible was present. Have you ever had your skin *grow* on you? That's what happened to me in these circumstances, but I would stand on guard while she went to the bathroom and then we'd go back to bed.

The ghost world is there regardless of what anybody says.

My mother used to tell me that spirits would follow me home if I came home late at night, and specially if I passed a cemetery. I'd come in and happily go to sleep but nobody else in the house could because somebody from the spirit world was bugging them.

To avoid this, my mother used to say "Don't forget to turn around at the door. Leave whatever you're bringing in out there."

We were supposed to stop at the door, face out and then back in through the door. This little ritual was meant to prevent the ghost people from following us into the house.

My brother never bought into any of this. He's very down-to-earth and always said, "You must be kidding to tell me these kinds of stories." He did not believe in any ghosts, spooks or spirits and today he is a medical specialist practicing in Guyana.

One day however, all this changed. He had gone to Switzerland and brought a very beautiful Swiss lace nightdress home for Mama. Typical of the age and time, she packed it away neatly in soft lavender paper and put it in the drawer, ready to wear if she ever had to go to the hospital.

She said, "If anything happens to me, you must give this nightdress to your daughter Louella." She was my brother's firstborn.

"Okay, sure," he said flippantly.

When Momma eventually died though, he brought the elegant nightdress home from the hospital and put it in a drawer. He was getting ready to come to Canada to meet up with his wife and kids.

As he packed he was talking to his closest friend. All of a sudden, as he told us later, Momma was sitting there with her shoulder-length hair, wearing her usual clothes, rocking back and forth and smiling. "Forget that!" he thought to himself.

He looked again and he could see her clear as day.

"Man, I've got a visitor," he said to his friend.

"What are you talking about?"

He told him.

My brother couldn't understand what was going on until he realized that when he packed, he had not packed the nightdress.

"Are you after the nightgown again?" he asked Momma.

He went upstairs, found it and put it in the suitcase. When he came back down, Momma was still sitting there.

"Are you happy now?" he asked. "I've packed the nightgown for Louella."

She smiled.

In the meantime his friend wondered what on earth was going on. When my brother turned his back, Momma was gone.

Later he told my sisters and me that he would never believe the stories of the spirits following us home from the graveyard but this, he said, "I saw this with my own eyes."

Now we always say, "Momma is the she-devil. She'll turn up forever. And she'll get you if you're not doing the right thing."

Once my youngest sister said, "Good Lord, that old lady came

……she was rocking back and forth

and bugged me all night."

When I was small I used to smell death. It was a very earthy smell, something like the peculiar smell of flowers at a funeral. When somebody died, they laid the person out and had a wake. At these times, I used to get this smell but didn't understand it. I mentioned it to one of my older girlfriends.

"That's the dead," she said. "That's how they smell."

I discovered if someone in our family was going to die, I would get that smell a couple of days beforehand but usually brushed it off. Then suddenly, someone would come to tell us that a relative had died. Years later, when I lived in Canada the same thing happened just before one of my aunts passed away.

Over the years, I learned to put this whole thing in its own perspective. It's a sort of sensitivity I have but I have no idea why.

THE GRASS LAKE INCIDENT: A PARANORMAL INVESTIGATOR CONFRONTS THE UNKNOWN ©

I became a paranormal investigator over twenty-five years ago, not out of some mild curiosity, but from a burning desire born out of two head-on collisions with paranormal reality that happened to me in the 1970s. The first occurred in the winter of 1971, while I was attending graduate school at the University of Vienna.

During the Christmas holiday, four companions and I decided to take a skiing holiday to Innsbruck in the Austrian Alps. We took the train from Vienna, but, typical students that we were, by the time we got to Innsbruck, we had spend most of our money on food and beer. None of us could afford lift tickets, so we ended up cross-country skiing over the Nordketten Ridge between Innsbruck and Kitzbuhl.

After about an hour we came to a break in the tree line and immediately noticed a metallic object in a ravine approximately 200 yards below us. The disc-shaped object, not over twenty feet in diameter, seemed to be quietly spinning. It behaved as if it were hiding from something, but occasionally the disc wobbled and caught the sunlight, which gave away its position. We took off our skis and started hiking down the side of the mountain, but the closer we got to the object, the faster and more steady it spun, until finally, it just disappeared in thin air or shot off so fast we were unable to see it leave.

Immediately, we all began rationalizing about the incident and eventually convinced ourselves we had been fooled by the reflection of the sun off some ice or snow in the darkened ravine. However, I had a feeling in my stomach that there was something not quite right about the whole incident and I decided to spend a little time researching UFO reports in the area. I soon discovered that Europe was in the middle of a "UFO flap," or flurry of sightings, that stretched along a line from Bolzano, Italy, through western Austria, and into Sweden. There were dozens of photographs taken in the Alps of saucer-shaped craft, and one biochemistry professor from the University of Innsbruck even reported seeing humanoid figures standing alongside one of the grounded objects. Whatever was happening, it was a lot more than just sunlight reflecting off the snow.

When I returned to the United States, I immediately became an investigator for nearly every national UFO organization in existence at the time. I was determined to find out what was going on. Convinced I was dealing with hardware from space, I usually tried to avoid cases that involved contactees or alien abductions, simply because they did not contain the quality of physical evidence for which I was searching. Still, being the new guy with these organizations sometimes meant I was forced to investigate cases I would have rather avoided.

One such case took place in Grass Lake, Illinois, a small farming community on the Illinois-Wisconsin border. Starting in July 1973, three separate families (eleven individuals) from around the tiny lake were calling the police and fire departments reporting strange orange lights in the sky. The authorities responded over a dozen times, and on several occasions officers witnessed the lights, but realizing there was not much they could do to keep them away, they stopped responding to UFO sightings at the lake in 1975. At that point, the families banded together and contacted a number of UFO organizations, including two with which I was associated, the Centre for UFO Studies at Northwestern University and the International UFO Registry, a group I had joined while still in Europe.

I spent several days at the lake interviewing the various families and trying to sort through their bizarre experiences. One of the witnesses, Nancy Hansen, was keeping a logbook of everything that happened. A few assorted entries from her journal describe how innocently things began:

July 1-3, 1973. We went to the other side of the lake and talked to a witness who said it looked like a white light with a red rim. He had a lot of close sightings of the UFOs. He lives on the highest hill in that area.

August 3, 1974. We now have one right over the lake. On closer inspection with binoculars, it resembles a fried egg—a dark dome with solid light rim, bordered with red and green lights. Five witnesses watched it. It showed up every night and stayed until unknown time. Another family that lived on the lake got a close view each night from their yard.

July 21, 1975. My daughter Kathy called me to the front room door to look at the orange light in the sky. I took my time because I thought it was Venus reflecting the sun. But it wasn't. It was the size of a tennis ball at arm's length and started pulsating orange and white very fast. Then after a few minutes it started northwest and faded just before it got to the trees.

Before long, the sightings of the orange UFOs became a nightly occurrence. About that time, a local New Age group they had asked for help suggested they try group psychic communication with the unidentifiable lights. These efforts were deemed successful when some of the objects started blinking on and off in apparent response to group concentration efforts and later even blinked some messages back in International Morse Code, which the group had taught them telepathically. However, with the escalation in contact and communication, a lot of very strange things began to happen in the homes of witnesses.

The poltergeist effects included loud knocking and clawing sounds, sounds of things falling but nothing dropping, sudden foul odors such as sulfur and fish, lights and radios turning on by themselves, clocks turning ahead, furniture falling over, unexplainable variations in room temperature, and the disappearance and later return of common personal objects such as pens, flashlights, house-slippers, and purses. One family reported that a bedroom pillow had suddenly begun taking moisture out of the air until it became totally saturated and began soaking the bed. They then took the pillow into the front room and removed the pillowcase, at which time the pillowcase started drying but the whole room turned ice cold.

All three families reported instances when their houses would "bounce" up and down, shaking from the foundation up for no apparent reason; and one house had deep, claw-like indentations made over one whole side of its cedar siding. At that same address on Thanksgiving Day 1973, a resident had fired a full round of bullets at a hairy, humanoid creature he had seen prowling near the house.

Other elusive humanoid shapes were reportedly actually roaming through the homes of those who saw the UFOs. Again I quote from Nancy's journal:

November 17, 1973, 10:00 P.M. I mistook a dark shadow for my husband. It was standing at the foot of my bed. I called out my husband's name and it walked around to his side of the bed. I called his name again and reached up to turn on the light, but when I did he was gone. My husband says that he did not come in or even go near the bedroom at that time.

February 8, 1974. While my daughter Pam was in bed, something pulled the covers down to her knees and gently pinched her toes like it had a claw instead of a hand. She thought it was trying to pull her out of bed. She said it got real cold just before and while this happened. She was so scared she stayed up the rest of the night.

August 5, 1974. Jo called from her new house to say that invisible chains were drug up and down her stairs. Later a small, gold-metallic suited blond walked through the bedroom, stopped a minute, and then went through some invisible door.

May 2, 1975. Sue followed a woman into Kathy's room thinking she was following Pam to ask her a question. When she got inside she was the only one in the room. She was really upset by it.

May 12, 1975. A pen and pack of gum was taken right in front of my husband's eyes in the bedroom as he was getting ready for work. Did he get mad! He yelled so much at them that when he went into the front room to go, they were by the front door where he couldn't miss them. It wasn't the pen or gum, it was the frustration that finally made him get so mad. He is a nervous wreck from them forever taking his stuff.

August 26, 1975. Pam got up last night and as she came up the hallway, she saw a man standing outside our front room window. At first she said she thought it was a gorilla but then she could see it was a man with pincer-like hands. She ducked into the bathroom and when she came out it was gone.

Not long afterwards, the families started discerning what the elusive humanoid shapes invading their homes looked like. At first they could see them clearly only in mirrors, but eventually were able to look at them directly. There seemed to be three basic types of these alien entities. The scariest were the wild Bigfoot types, which seemed to be under the control of the most sinister of the beings: tall, reptilian creatures with greenish scales and six-fingered claws. The other type was short, gray-skinned creatures with fat heads and bright, wide eyes that elongated along the sides of their heads.

Once they were able to see the creatures, the reptilian entities started chasing them even more frequently, and all the homes had examples of horrible scratch marks on the walls and furniture. The New Age group proposed that the aliens represented two opposing forces battling to gain control over their lives. This seemed comforting to offer the witnesses, who now at least saw some purpose in the demonic activity into which they had been thrown.

Of course, I was taking all this with a grain of salt. After all, this was well over twenty-five years ago, long before abduction reports became common and Harvard professors were staking their reputations that they were really happening. At the time, most researchers, who were desperately searching for scientific credibility, wanted to downplay such incidents.

One evening, I was sitting at the kitchen table going over Nancy's journals with her. Her husband sat staring at the television in the living room, so confused or terrified that he just stopped talking about the goings-on in his home. With her husband's condition rapidly deteriorating and both her daughters terrified to go to bed at night, I asked Nancy why they just did not pack up and move away. In a moment of personal honesty, she admitted that none of the families had enough money to leave the lake. Their homes were over a hundred years old and had been passed down from generation to generation. They were originally simple farmers and now had to work menial jobs just to make ends meet.

As if confirming its age, the house seemed to settle a little. I assumed it must have been something in the foundation, but seconds later there was a loud thump on the outside wall. Thinking something had hit the side of the house, I jumped up, ran over to a half-open dining room window, and stuck my head out. I turned my head to my right and could see these claw marks actually forming on the wood siding outside. It was cedar siding and the invisible claws were digging in about an eighth of an inch, revealing the fresh red wood underneath. Before I glanced out, approximately four inches had formed, but when I started watching, the claws seemed to dig in deeper and went on for another five inches.

Well, there was no way anyone could have faked that, and quite honestly, I was a little scared. There were no trees anywhere, the long driveway was empty, and the pitch of the roof was too steep for anyone to hide there. It was simply too much for my mind to grasp at the moment, and all I wanted to do was be alone and think about it. I did not exactly run screaming from the house, but I quickly excused myself without telling anyone what I saw and headed for my car, which I had parked at the side of the road.

Once in my car, I felt as if my brain was on fire trying to figure out explanations for what I saw. Then, as I started down the dark blacktop road, my headlights started blinking on and off in Morse code fashion. I pulled to the side of the road and watched in amazement as the lights danced on and off with my ammeter remaining dead centre steady, as if my lights were drawing their power from another source. Even after I turned off the switch, they continued flashing. Finally, after about five minutes, they stopped, and I pulled the switch on, after which they worked correctly all the way back to Chicago.

The next day, when I took the car in to be checked by a mechanic, he could find nothing wrong with the wiring, but did discover that the left hand side of the car had been magnetized. One of his screwdrivers stuck to one side but not the other. Furthermore, a Geiger counter I had in the trunk was pegged out full scale and ruined, even though it was turned off.

I returned to Grass Lake two weeks later with a team of investigators ready to stake out the lake, but by that time the families were in real crisis and had contacted a local church group. They told the witnesses that they were brought demons into their homes by their "sinful" acts and had already performed an exorcism in one of the houses. We were asked not to come back. I did take photos and wrote up the case in the *Journal of UFOlogy,* but the case was simply too far out to be taken seriously.

I visited Nancy about three years later, and we sat together at the same kitchen table where my encounter with the Other Side had begun. I looked at her temples and noticed the dime-sized scars of electroshock therapy; she had suffered a nervous breakdown. Her husband had left her, and her family had disowned her, and I could offer her no real comfort. From cases like these, the organizations have since learned that experiencers of paranormal events need and deserve all the investigative and psychological help we can give them. We cannot behave like parasites living off their experiences anymore. We have to realize that by entering into their innermost feelings, we have genuine responsibilities to treat them fairly and help them work through these belief-shattering encounters.

I never saw any UFOs or creatures at Grass Lake, but what I did see has left an indelible mark on me too. I am no longer a "hardware man," nor do I believe earth is being invaded from outer space. Instead, we are being invaded from inner space, from realms in our own minds which lie waiting, ignored for too long. There is an unsuspected connection between human consciousness and reality, a connection which the longer we rail to acknowledge, the harder it will intrude into our everyday existence.

Dennis Hauck, Paranormal investigator, author, consultant, U.S.

SKULL COVE ©

Following is an astral experience of mine, showing the typical structure of the astral planes and their entrances. The astral planes are very aptly named as 'planes.' They are set out like the pages in a book and these pages/planes appear, from the astral, to be several miles apart. The divisions between astral planes appear to be quite visually distinct. In between the planes are areas that appear to be buffer zones, separating individual astral planes from others. These buffer zones vary in appearance but have distinct geometric similarities. Some of these buffer zones are dark and some are coloured, but all appear to be featureless and empty. Passing through these buffer zones is a bit like floating through a series of huge connected tanks, each filled with different coloured water, with spectacular geometric patterned barriers dividing each astral plane.

This projection happened at about 1 P.M. I did no energy work or meditation prior to it as I was intending to have a nap, not a projection. I was resting well but, although I was extremely tired, could not fall asleep (too much coffee maybe), and I began to see with astral sight through my closed eyelids, so decided to go astral for a while. I projected out of my body using the quick ROPE method and staggered free of my body. I literally staggered, feeling weak and having little directional control over my astral body. I floated with some difficulty through the wall of my room. As I passed through I felt a tingling, electrical type of buzzing and heard a slight, Velcrolike, ripping sound as I did. I could see the inside of the wall very clearly and brightly lit, the plaster coating over concrete and the texture of the internal bricks, etc., as I passed through it. I staggered towards the main room like a drunkard, intending to see if I could make my nephew, Matte, aware of me by passing through his body and giving him goose bumps.

Because of my lack of control, which I suspect was caused by being too close to my awake physical body, and possibly by too quick an exit, I decided to get out of the house for a while. I staggered into the spare bedroom and fell through the window into the front yard.

I shot up into the sky and headed towards the beach, just over a mile away, feeling much better once I was airborne. It was a glorious sunny day with brilliant blue sky and very little cloud. Lifting higher I willed myself to go faster and faster, increasing speed dramatically. The world blurred around me and I quickly found myself somewhere in the astral planes. At first I was in total darkness (possibly what some people call the void) but soon moved through this into a brighter coloured area. I could see blue, like the early evening sky, all around me, but directly behind me was only darkness, a black featureless void. Spread out before me, several miles below, was a vast astral plane entrance covered in grid lines. Every square of the grid-lined structure was filled with the same spectacular, multicoloured geometric pattern. This was the doorway, the entrance to an astral plane. It spread out beneath me as far as I could see in all directions. It was like looking at the earth from a great height, seeing an infinite number of small, multi-coloured, patterned fields, all exactly the same size, shape, colour and pattern.

It is extremely difficult to describe such an enormous spectacle as this, as in the physical world there is very little to use for a fair comparison. The grid-lined pattern of this dimensional entrance was like an endless checkerboard of squares, each one filled with exactly the same brightly coloured intricate pattern, repeated endlessly as far as I could see. I was excited and awe struck by this spectacular geometric beauty. With no hesitation I flew straight for it, diving swiftly down towards the pattern. A tingling rush of energy flooded up my spine and I screamed out joyfully, as loud as I could "Geronimooooooo! Heeeeeee! Haaaaaaaaaaaa!" and heard my voice booming loud and clear throughout the astral.

As I approached the patterned entrance the individual squares grew steadily larger, but remained sharply distinct until the last moment as I plunged through one of them. There was no sensation of impact but the transition was dramatic. I found myself in what felt like deep-blue water. Visibility was extremely good and I could see several hundred meters in all directions. There were small bubbles and tiny bits of floating matter all around me to indicate I was indeed under water. I headed at a slight angle towards a lighter area I guessed to be the surface. Movement caught my eye and far off I saw a group of huge fish. I moved closer and saw a school of several enormous fish. They were round, flat and brightly coloured, very much like tropical discus fish, but these appeared to be much larger than the biggest whales on Earth. Swimming amongst these fancy behemoths were sharks, but these were tiny compared to the big fish - like minnows amongst giants. One of the great fish looked at me as I flew through the school, and watched me calmly with one great, friendly eye the size of a VW Beetle as I passed close by it. I sensed intelligence and friendliness coming from the fish.

I surfaced through lively ocean waves and flew high into a glorious indigo sky. There were two suns shining down upon me, one large and orange and one small and yellow. A few miles away I could see a small bay lined with creamy yellow sands and surf. Jutting out from the shore at the left of this a massive skull-shaped rock looking to be a couple of hundred meters high caught my attention. Spinning around I noticed a fleet of seven large sailing ships. They were big wooden ships, high in the prow and stern, low amidships and square-rigged in a way I had never seen before. Seeing people crawling like ants upon their decks, I dived towards them as they tacked, all turning in unison, sails and tackle cracking and spray blasting from their strangely curved bows as they ploughed through the water and heaved into the rolling waves. I came to rest on the high aft deck of the lead ship near the ship's wheel on the stern. I had spent several years in the merchant navy during my youth, so knew something about ships.

It looked like a fairly normal ship, but everything appeared slightly different from what I knew of large sailing ships.

The men looked vaguely European, were dark-haired, tanned, barefoot and dressed in rough, drab-grey shirts with brown pants cut off at the knees. They had beaded rope headbands and white scarves tied around their waists. I approached the ship's wheel and saw an attractive brown hairdo on a woman perched next to it on a large bale of what looked like wool or cotton. She'd been staring at me since I'd landed, but turned her head quickly when she saw me look at her. The only woman on deck, she was barefoot like the men but wore a knee length shift of coarse white linen. This was tied at the waist with a large, braided leather belt, her loose hair hanging halfway to her waist. A small, intricately carved, bone-handled knife was thrust into her belt. She touched this briefly as I approached her, then folded her arms tightly in front of her and glared at me.

I quickly looked down at myself to make sure I was dressed. Fair enough, I was wearing shorts and T-shirt, my standard astral garb. I spoke to the woman very respectfully. She quickly turned away, looking very annoyed. I moved around her so she'd have to look at me again, but she turned her head again, hopped off the bale and walked quickly away towards a raised wooden hatchway. I called after her and she muttered something derisive sounding back at me before disappearing through it. I couldn't make out what she'd said, but she sounded very annoyed. I approached a few of the deck hands as they went about the business of running the ship, but they all dropped their eyes or turned away as I approached. This was most peculiar, I thought, everyone could see me but no one seemed to want anything to do with me. I felt very unwelcome there and soon left the ship.

I circled around the fleet for while and then took a long sweeping pass over the shoreline. Landing on the skull shaped rock I quickly explored it. It looked as if it had been carved out of white limestone, but was well weathered and obviously quite ancient. I saw no one and nothing of real interest on the shore or the rock and everything appeared very peaceful. I debated whether to look for another astral realm hereabouts or to move on to another plane entirely. I decided to take up my original trajectory and, hopefully, pass into the next astral plane. I hoped it would be friendlier and more interesting than this one. Lifting off again, I flapped my arms and picked up speed, soon leaving the strange shoreline and unfriendly fleet far behind me. Up ahead a darker area came into view, like a growing shadowy haze on the horizon. Pretty soon this engulfed me and I found myself in darkness again, and then in another featureless but green void-like area. Ahead of me appeared another spectacular checkerboard plane. It had different colours and patterns but was essentially the same type of structure as the first astral plane entrance. I felt my body calling me then, and everything began to slow down and blur, as if I were moving through thick mud. There was a sudden multicoloured blur and a fizzy crackling sensation and I found myself back in my body. The projection had ended.

Robert Bruce, internationally respected mystic and author, Australia.

ξ CHAPTER THREE ξ

ANIMATED ANIMALS

Animals are such agreeable friends —
they ask no questions, they pass no criticisms.
George Eliot (1819 – 1880)

Oh the magic and awesomeness of animals!

If I close my eyes, I can easily bring to mind the sweet smell and furry feel of newborn kittens in a loft of newly-mown hay, kittens with their tightly shut eyes, their razor sharp little nails, and their squeaky little meows. Mystery and enchantment rolled into one.

There have been many stories of cats who curl up on the bed beside a dying person. One who strolled into the prestigious New England Journal of Medicine is Oscar, a two-year-old grey and white brindled cat who grew up and lives at a nursing home in Rhode Island. So far, Oscar has made over 25 accurate predictions simply by curling up and purring beside the chosen person some 2 – 4 hours prior to the event and refusing to leave until the person has died.

There are many stories of both dogs and cats that run to the front door about half an hour before a beloved owner comes home, even when the routines vary. British biologist and author Rupert Sheldrake "explores the psychic power of animals and its implication for human consciousness" according to Renaissance Magazine.[xi] *Sheldrake, a Fellow of the Institute of Noetic Sciences in California, has examined how dogs know when their owners are coming home or how they get excited when their owners even think of taking them for a walk!*

Other scientists are conducting research into the ability of dogs being able to sniff out prostate or bladder cancers with interesting results.

Remember the story of that wonderful pig lying down in the middle of the road until someone stopped and she could lead them to the aid of her stricken mistress? Whether the pig was a Wessex Saddleback, a Hampshire, a Poland China or any of the ten other breeds of pigs, I don't know, but imagine the astounding love residing in her -- a little pig!

Who is to say why we have the pets we do and why they love us so. Sometimes we choose them and other times they choose us. Scientists tell us there are more than one-and-a-half million named and classified animals.

It is my opinion that animals are one of the greatest gifts we have been given in this wonderful world of ours.

CALICO CATS ©

How wonderful to experience a gift that comes wrapped in love, touched by the Divine, and tied with a multicoloured ribbon of red, black, and white superstitious belief.

Not once but three times.

My friend Bernadette was raised in a close-knit and loving family where she and her younger brother enjoyed the affection of parents and many extended family members. They rarely had to look outside the family circle for warmth, companionship or friendship. One aunt was particularly special to Bernadette, as was her grandmother.

Bernadette loves nature and seems to have a special gift for identifying the call of a bird and she knows the name of all beautiful, even obscure flowers.

And she loves cats.

Most people have at least one superstition about cats and Bernadette is no different. She has always believed that if someone who loves you very much dies, that person will send you a gift in the form of a cat for love and protection. From the Other Side.

A number of years ago, Bernadette and her family lived in the country. When her much loved brother died after a lengthy illness, Ballou, the calico cat from next door, moved in.

Ballou, a pretty female with a red, black and white coat, was just under one year old. No amount of coaxing would persuade her to return to her own home. When Bernadette went on vacation, the recalcitrant calico was returned to her despairing owners but Ballou was waiting on the doorstep when Bernadette returned.

Ballou was a warm and loving cat who brought solace and comfort. Bernadette felt she had an inner wisdom. When Ballou became pregnant, it was only after she was firmly ensconced beside Bernadette's bed that she delivered her litter.

An excellent mother, she taught her little ones in kitten ways. Early one spring Ballou and one of her own daughters each had a litter about a week apart. The daughter rejected one of her kittens and put it in with Ballou's kittens.

One day Bernadette looked at Ballou and said, "Are you going to put up with this?"

Ballou thoughtfully gazed at her, then picked up the rejected kitten, carried it over to the daughter's box and affectionately licked the daughter and all the kittens including the rejected one. The rejected one was tenderly accepted into the fold.

Years later Bernadette and her family were living in the city when she received word that her favourite aunt had died. Within weeks, a second calico appeared, seemingly from nowhere. Another female, also about a year old. Ballou by this time was quite old and no longer wanted to cuddle. Alley-cat cuddled Bernadette and provided her with a sense of serenity and peace.

This spring, four months after sweet Grandma died, Portia arrived out of nowhere and simply sat on the porch. At first, Bernadette was hesitant in taking in yet another calico, especially one who was guilelessly loving and relatively aggressive.

But Portia has made a place for herself with her joyful antics and invariable cheerfulness. When I hear Bernadette and her kids laughing, I know that Portia is either turning somersaults or running up and down the stairs after her favourite red ball.

Ancient folklore tells us that Japanese fishermen paid huge sums of money for a calico to sail the seas with them. The cat's job was to protect the crew from ancestral ghosts and the ship from storms.

The Celts considered it a good omen if a calico cat decided to settle in someone's home.

Were Ballou, Alley-Cat and Portia sent from the Other Side?

I don't know. But Bernadette is grateful for the calicos and the gifts they bring.

Love comes in many forms.[xii]

DARK PREMONITIONS

My sister was expecting her first baby on Saturday, June 19th, in the early 1950's. She and her husband lived in the city some forty miles away. Because she had been in hospital for the past three weeks with some medical problems, we did not know whether she would deliver early or not, so I just waited to hear from them.

My husband and I were farming at the time and had a lot of machinery in a shed near the barn. Early one Saturday morning, my husband had just opened the chicken-house and the hens and roosters scattered every which way. I took my pail and was on my way to do the milking while the cows were still in the barn. As I walked past the seeding-drill, a hen flew up on it. She turned and turned until she faced me squarely. Then she crowed a long deep crow, louder even than any of the roosters.

I didn't think anything of it but my husband had heard that this was a very bad omen and tried to chase the hen away, but she kept turning to face me as I walked by. Her staring unnerved me, but with three kids and lots of chores to do, I soon forgot the incident.

That same evening I went to get the cows, three black-and-white Holsteins and two red Guernsey's, from the pasture where they were grazing during the day. For a gate, we used two strands of wire across the gateway. We usually undid only the top wire and the cows had learned to step over the bottom one.

However the bottom wire was already opened and lying on the ground, so I loosened the top one and put it down on the ground too. As the cows made their way out of the enclosure, one of the Holsteins dragged one end of the bottom wire a short distance but as she continued, the wire was left behind.

When I got to the barn with them, I was surprised to see the Holstein's foot bleeding just above the hoof but it did not look like an ordinary wire cut. It looked like the scarring and bleeding on the picture of the Sacred Heart of Mary that we had in our kitchen. I checked the other cows' hind feet and they all had the same kind of scarring and bleeding.

Bewildered, I re-examined the extent of the injury on the first cow, but now there was nothing to see. No scars, no blood. Not knowing what to make of all this, I ignored it.

The next morning, on Sunday, we drove to Toronto to see my sister in the hospital. On arrival, we were devastated to learn that both she and her baby had died the previous day, on Saturday the 19th of June. I was heart-broken. Because we did not have telephone service at that time, my brother had sent us a telegram on that fateful day informing us of her death, but the telegram didn't arrive until two days later, the day before we buried her.

Only later did I think of the crowing hen and the bleeding scars on the heels of the cows. I could not understand these things and derived no comfort from them.

HOWLING DOGS

My mother always used to say that howling dogs were a premonition of impending death, at least in the English village where she grew up. So if someone was very ill, dogs supposedly howled the entire night before the person died.

Here in Ontario, I certainly had never heard anyone else say anything like this and I dismissed these old British yarns as nothing more than folklore. Dogs howl for many, many reasons and I seriously doubted that they wailed as a premonition of someone dying.

One warm Saturday afternoon in the summer, when my son Jonathan was only about three weeks old, my husband and I were leisurely strolling downtown, pushing our brand new baby in his buggy. We ambled down to King & James Streets, through the busy section of the Right House block, where in the middle, there was a Woolworth's store. Saturdays were always teeming with shoppers and this lovely sunny day was no exception.

Suddenly, seemingly from nowhere, this big dark dog ran out of the crowd, stopped and lay down barely two feet away from the front of the buggy, put his head back, and howled like a wolf. Then he ran off and disappeared into the crowd once more.

My husband and I both said, "Where did that dog come from?" and then, "Where did he go?" because he just seemed to vanish.

We thought it odd that he appeared without warning and then just as abruptly disappeared. Although there were a lot of people there, we couldn't figure out why we didn't see him going down the

A DARK DOG

street. The whole incident was peculiar. and eerily out of place.

However we were soon distracted by the crowds and the nice day and we thought nothing more of it. We went on up to my parents' home in the west end of the city, eager to show off our new baby boy once more.

My father, a healthy strapping man, was walking down the street on his way home from work as we arrived, but we could see that something was different, something was wrong. He looked dreadful and generally unwell. We convinced my mother to call the doctor who decided to put him in the hospital for some tests "because he looked tired."

That night my father died.

Neither my husband nor I thought of the incident with the dog at the time, but we were to recall it later. If there hadn't been the two of us there, I would have sworn that I hadn't seen the dog because it was that unusual. But both my husband and I did see him.

Whether there's anything to my mother's old English tale or not I don't know, but I've always wondered about it.

HOT AND COLD

Several years ago, my husband Michael and I moved from our twentieth-story apartment to a lovely old house out in the country. We were delighted at the prospect of working in our own flower and vegetable gardens and sunning in the huge back yard. Of course no move would be complete without Billy, our tubby twelve-year-old tabby whom we loved dearly. Every night since he was a little kitten, he slept at the foot of our bed.

We moved into our new home the first of December amidst the usual truckloads of furniture and boxes. Moving day was very long and frustrating, partly because of the six inches of fresh snow that made driving hazardous. In the evening Michael suggested I take a nice hot bubble bath while he finished the last chore of the day, which was cleaning the glass window on the back door.

I luxuriated in the steamy bath, soaking my sore joints when Michael stuck his head around the corner.

"What's the problem?" I asked, not appreciating even the slightest disturbance in my bubbly reverie.

"Did you just get out of the tub?" he asked.

"No."

"You didn't go to the living room?"

"No I didn't," I snapped. "In case you didn't notice, I'm having a bath."

"Okay," he mumbled and closed the door.

Later at the dinner table, I asked him what that was all about.

He looked at me with this funny look in his eye, and then hesitantly said, "While I was cleaning the back window, I saw this white form slip through the hall and into the living room. I thought you stepped out of the bath to have one of your bloody cigarettes. You've done it before."

"I never moved."

"I know you didn't," he said feebly.

That night we both felt a frigid chill in the hallway leading into our bedroom, but we were too drained to give it much thought. What did give us pause was that Billy refused to sleep with us! I thought something was wrong with him and carried him into the bedroom. But he yelped and tore out of there so fast that I was grateful he was de-clawed. Nothing we could say or do would make him come into the bedroom. He slept on the living room couch that night.

For the next few days, Michael and I worked hard at organizing our new home. On the weekend, we were tired and made a pact to go to bed early. In readiness, I turned on both of our electric blankets to have our bed toasty warm. But then Sharon and Tom, close friends of ours, dropped in unexpectedly. So much for an early night, we thought.

But I could see Michael's pride as he showed Tom around the grounds and I was equally happy taking Sharon on a grand tour of the house. I told her about the "ghost" that Michael had seen, and how Billy refused to come into our bedroom. Sharon said she too felt a chill in the back hall.

After some nice hot apple cider and crackers and cheese, they left and we finally popped into bed. But my side was ice cold. My electric blanket had been turned off. Sure that either Tom or Sharon had played a trick on us, I called them the next morning to give them a blast, but they vehemently denied touching the controls on either of the electric blankets.

By this time, Michael and I were convinced that we had a resident ghost in our house. We decided to have a little chat with her.

"You're welcome to stay here with us," I said loudly into the frigid hallway. "But please don't spook our cat Billy. Leave him alone. Okay?"

I half expected an answer but none was forthcoming and nothing changed despite our repeated pleas. The air in the hallway remained icy cold and Billy refused to venture into that part of the house. He continued to sleep in the living room every night.

A few days before Christmas, the son and daughter-in-law of the old lady that used to live here came by for a visit. They were pleased to see what we had done with the house in such a short time and enjoyed a glass of Christmas cheer with us. There was no mention of any strange goings-on but they did say that the old lady had died in her house.

After they left, we noticed that the hallway had suddenly warmed up. And for the first time since we moved in, Billy came to bed with us, acting like nothing had ever happened.

I think the apparition my husband saw when we first moved in was the ghost of the old lady. I never saw her but I don't think she liked me because she had turned *my* electric blanket off. When the son and daughter-in-law came to visit, I think they took her with them. That's my idea anyhow.

ACCIDENTAL VISITOR

Tomato picking and tomato canning season was always a very busy one but my husband and I usually decided to do both. While the kids were at school, I picked the tomatoes and Steve drew the wagonload of brimming red hampers with our big green tractor to the canning factory, driving at a relatively slow speed on the dirt road that ran alongside the canal in front of our property. Travelling on the paved road on the opposite side with a full wagonload of freshly picked tomatoes would have been foolhardy and dangerous. We lived a short distance away from the canning factory where Steve also worked, so he was able to come home for lunch with the empty wagon and then return in time for the afternoon shift. When the pear season started, it was twice as busy and Steve was often asked to work after supper. By then, the days were getting shorter and dusk would descend around nine P.M.

One day Steve said beets were being trucked in too, so he thought he would not get home until 10 P.M. I had all the evening chores in the barn finished and was waiting for him to come home when Sandy, our protective collie, barked loudly. I looked out the kitchen window and saw a man walking up to the porch steps. I started to go out to see who it was and then decided to wait until he knocked.

But there was no knocking at the door, so I went to see what the delay was. Much to my amazement, Sandy was just about to go into his favourite little hideaway underneath the porch. I couldn't believe it. He would never leave me alone if someone were there. And now he had gone under the porch to his usual sleeping place, as if he didn't have a care in the world.

I walked down the steps to where I had seen the man walking, but there was no one there. I went further down the path leading to the dirt road and no one was there either. Wondering if someone was hiding by the house, I looked behind the rain-barrel at the corner of the house, the most likely hiding spot. No one there either.

Sandy had come out to investigate what I was doing, but he was obviously unconcerned. I glared at the open, empty garage that was some distance from the house, looking for some sign of the man, but there was none. Puzzled, I went back to the house while Sandy returned to his favourite spot.

By now it was getting quite dark and when Steve finally came home, he drove the car directly into the garage. I went out to meet him and he pointed to a tree on the other side of the canal, just around the curve in the road.

"See those lights over there?"

I peered into the darkness and saw flashing police lights and the shadowed hoist of a tow-truck.

"There was a bad accident there."

He explained that a young man had been driving his father's car, apparently fell asleep at the wheel, and smashed head-on into that tree. His car caught fire. Somebody pulled him out but he died.

I shivered. Was that the young man Sandy barked at, the one I saw walking toward the house, on the beginning of a ghostly journey? Clearly he meant no harm. I know Sandy would have protected me from anyone, real or ghostly.

A KITTEN FOR CHRISTMAS

Christmas was always a magical time when we were kids. It was really an extension of the exuberance of the rest of our childhood days. My two older brothers and I loved the open sky of our farm, the endless summers, the animals -- horses, cows, pigs, cats and dogs -- and the good wholesome farm food. We had our own chickens, vegetables, and fruit including a huge apple orchard with every imaginable kind of apple including Northern Spies, Greening and Snows.

The month preceding the Christmas when I was five years old had been bitterly cold with numerous snowstorms. For me it meant more days that my brothers got to stay home and play instead of going to school. That particular December also meant more of the severe colds that I had always been prone to.

Every negative has a flip positive side, and for me being too ill to go outside to play meant that I was allowed to go to the door of our front porch and call "Here kitty, kitty, kitty! Here kitty, kitty, kitty!"

Within moments my cat ("they were always *your* cats" as one of my brothers recently said) would come barrelling out of the barn, up the hill, through the open door to the porch, and then make a bee-line for the wood-burning stove in the kitchen and snuggle in under it. It was the only time my mother allowed animals of any kind in the house.

Our huge country kitchen was enormous and easily welcomed an antique golden velvet loveseat with matching armchair and rocker that my father had purchased at an auction sale. It was on this loveseat that I recuperated while watching my mother go about her daily tasks, including baking apple pies. But the very best part was when my warmed-up kitten crawled out from under the stove, jumped up on the loveseat and cuddled next to me. Absolute heaven.

My father was a trapper in the wintertime and because he was a compassionate man, he never missed one day, so that the animals would not needlessly suffer. Early every morning he walked miles to the Grand River which lay a good distance on the other side of the railway tracks that were themselves one full field back of the house. He always said he was going "back of the track." From the kitchen window I would see him coming back home, carrying heavy sacks full of muskrats and mink that had been caught in the traps set on the riverbank.

He skinned them in the barn. He hung them up by their tails, incised circles first around the tail and then the hind legs, and made precise cuts between these circles. Then the pelts were skinned down with great care so as not to create any holes in the fur. The carcasses were thrown into a huge pit behind the barn and the skins were stretched inside out to dry on special wire racks. The wider racks were for the muskrat skins and the longer thinner ones were for the mink. The fur buyers would come to our house every couple of weeks or so and buy the pelts after some haggling over prices.

In late November the cat we had went off on a mousing venture and never returned. Now as I lay on the loveseat, hacking and coughing, barely able to make a sound because my throat was so sore, I missed having a warm furry ball next to me.

My mom and dad explained that there were no kittens to be had in December, but in the spring, "you can have any kitten you want." But I wanted a kitten now. I *needed* a kitten for Christmas.

As the magic of Christmas drew near, my brothers and I decorated the green pine tree that my dad had cut and we strung popcorn on strings and added them to the other colourful decorations. We wrote our letters to Santa Claus.

…I *needed* a kitten for Christmas

In keeping with our Ukrainian tradition, as soon as the first star came out, we began our special Christmas Eve supper. My dad had already fed the cows and horses in the barn. Under the table was hay from the barn, to honour that first Christmas in a manger, so long ago. We started our supper with *"kutya,"* an extraordinary wheat dish served only on Christmas Eve. We had a total of twelve meatless dishes for that special meal, all made without butter or dairy products.

When we finished, we listened to thrilling radio accounts of Santa Claus with his sleigh and eight tiny reindeer, being spotted first here, then there, coming closer and closer to our house. We left a glass of milk and some homemade cookies for Santa. The excitement was too much for us and finally, on the longest night of the year, we fell asleep at last.

At five in the morning, my brothers and I woke up as if by design and we discovered that the milk and cookies were gone. We ran into the living room and amazingly, under the Christmas tree were so many wondrous presents that we couldn't believe our eyes.

But there was no kitten. "I asked Santa for a kitten," I said tears streaming down my face, "but he's not here yet."

"There are no kittens for Santa now either," my mother said softly. "You'll get one as soon as spring comes."

"You'll have your kitten before you know it," my dad added.

"But I asked Santa," I said. I knew in my heart that Santa answered all his letters. What could have happened?

Soon I was distracted by the joy of the day. After an early breakfast, my oldest brother went out to the barn to help my mother with some chores and my dad said he was going "back of the track" to check the trap line.

"Don't go today," my mother urged. "Give yourself a rest. It *is* Christmas."

He shook his head. "It won't take long," he said.

My other brother and I amused ourselves with games and toys. One of my gifts was a china piggybank in the form of a gorgeous chocolate brown and tan teddy bear, with a slit in the top of his head. I loved it. And I loved my books, but I had a nagging feeling. Why hadn't Santa brought me the kitten? Had I done something very bad?

About an hour after the barn chores were done, we saw my dad coming back home. My mom and I were watching out the kitchen window, and as my dad made his usual way to the barn, he waved at my mom to come outside, pointing to his heavy winter coat and smiling. Surprised, she grabbed her coat and went to join him.

When they came back in the house, their faces were glowing. "Santa got your letter," my dad said. "He's just a little late."

And then, in the most magical moment of my life, my dad handed me a kitten! I kissed him and hugged my beautiful kitty and showed him the Christmas tree and my brothers and all our toys and the warm kitchen stove and the golden velvet loveseat. Christmas was perfect.

It wasn't until later that I noticed he was missing one of his legs. He had only three. He probably had been caught in one of the traps on the river some time earlier.

Out of despair and pain had come joy and happiness for both of us. I had that miraculous Christmas kitten for many years.

PHANTOM RACCOON

In a theatre called the CENTRE OF THE SQUARE, the *Phantom of the Opera* was playing and of course there was a lot of hype about this popular production.

During all this, somehow a ringed-tailed raccoon made its way into the theatre and the Animal Removal people were called to get it out and to make sure it did not come in again. The cast and crew generally felt that the show had enough special effects of its own without help from the animal kingdom.

The only catch was, no one could find an entry hole for the raccoon despite much serious searching. How it got into the theatre in the first place remained a mystery.

Did this masked beauty merely find a way to beat the high price of admission or did he feel a connection to the masked star of the performance. Who knows? Perhaps the raccoon simply wanted to audition for the starring role.

PHANTOM of the OPERA

BATS and BELLS

It was Christmas and the Kelly's had their house decorated, the gifts were bought and wrapped, the cookies and cakes were baked, and a magnificent Christmas tree in the living room was decorated with stars and angels and little silver bells and garlands of red and green.

One day, Mrs. Kelly saw a branch on the Christmas tree tremble. It was just the slightest of movements. She took a closer look, saw nothing, and dismissed it without another thought. Over the next couple of days, she periodically saw the same slight trembling of the tree branches. When she told her husband and kids about it, they examined the Christmas tree and found nothing. Jenny and Allan laughed and teased her. They told their dad, "Mom's seeing things."

To make things worse, Mrs. Kelly could hear the little silver bells tinkling every once in a while. Now the kids really laughed and told their dad, "Now Mom's hearing things, too."

Mrs. Kelly was beginning to think her husband and kids were right, that maybe she was losing it since she was hearing and seeing things that no one else did.

Then all of a sudden, late one evening when they were watching "Frosty the Snowman" on TV, a dark bat took flight out of the tree and whipped around the living room. Mr. Kelly, Jenny and Allan took cover, not understanding what was going on. When Mr.

Kelly finally identified the flying object as a bat, he called me, an expert in the removal of wildlife animals.

He told me they didn't have a previous history of bat problems. It's common for us to get repeat calls because bats always return to the same place, but this particular customer claimed he had never had anything in his attic or had any experience with bats in any way. This bat just showed up.

Often by the time I get there, and I tell my customers this, the bats are probably going to be gone. Other times they're in plain sight. If they're not, I know where to look because I'm familiar with typical bat behaviour and know where they like to hide. Their bones are extremely flexible and they can fit into a crack the size of a dime or even smaller. They simply flatten themselves out and fly in. These awesome animals don't need much space.

So I went in the middle of the night because that's when bats take flight. I was able to grab this one easily because it was flying around the bedroom. Usually I do it with Wildlife gloves on or sometimes I just toss a towel over the bat and scoop it up.

Jenny and Allan were scared out of their minds. They half-expected the bat to suck their blood out. Their parents weren't much better. I referred them to a fantastic book on bats that they could pick up at the library.

This bat was really a mystery though because nobody could explain how it got in. If the Kelly's had a history of bat problems, I could say, "Well, they've had them before!" But they hadn't and they had lived in the same house since it was built, years and years ago.

After I removed the bat, the Kelly's never had another one. This is strange, especially at Christmas time, when bats are in hibernation. The exact time they go into hibernation is not clear. It's usually when their food source of mosquitoes is gone but it's not like on Monday there are mosquitoes and on Tuesday there aren't.

My co-workers and I tried to solve the mystery but we were only able to offer a hypothesis. Bats are extra-ordinary animals that don't fly around when there are no mosquitoes. We wondered if the Christmas tree had been cut early enough, whether the bat might already have been hibernating in the tree, but it seemed unlikely. When trees are cut up north, they're wrapped tightly in burlap that might be cool and dark enough to be conducive to hibernation. Things happen with bats that make me shake my head, wondering how they ever could have happened.

It is true that bats can get tangled up in your hair. They're after the bugs that fly around your head. Their ultrasonic radar device, or echolocation system, is very advanced but when you start batting the air with your hands, you cause the air currents to move and the bats become disoriented. If you were to stand perfectly still and not move while a bat was flying around your head, it would fly within centimetres of your hair and not get tangled up.

When I exclude bats from a home, I tell my customers that I'm not relocating the bats because that's impossible. Bats always go back home. So I say, "This bat will come back here, so let's give it a den site by putting up a bat house to use instead of your house."

A bat house is a little larger than a birdhouse. It's quite long and comes in different sizes. Old barn wood makes the best material. It's probably two feet high, a foot wide, and six inches deep. Inside are wooden slats for the bats to roost on. The house has to face southwest for optimum sun to control the environment by heating the wood. Bats enter their house through the open bottom. Wild Bird Clinics have some exceptionally attractive designer bat houses available.

There are 940 species of bats, but in Canada there are primarily only two different species, the Big Brown Bat (*eptesicus fuscus)* and the Little Brown Bat (myotis lucifungus). The Big Browns migrate to warmer climates and then return to the same area. The Little Browns stay and colonize and hibernate within attics and walls. If you were to tag them with a tracking device, you would discover that they always go back to the exact same house.

They have a life expectancy of over thirty years. Each female bat gives birth to one bat each year. They have no fertility problems and in the odd case, like humans, they'll give birth to twins. The females store the sperm inside themselves over winter and when they cycle in the spring, they release the sperm and become impregnated.

I have a real interest in these unusual animals. They're the only mammals that can attain true flight. Currently I'm trying to lure them to my farm where there's a good food source because I have a horrendous problem with mosquitoes and the livestock are conducive to attracting bugs.

Bats have never been introduced to my area, but to be perfectly honest, I don't know why I can't get them to come. They're probably a bit like red martens, the little birds that won't come right away. You have to entice them.

DOLPHIN THERAPY ©

For more many years, we at the *Dolphin Society* have been running the *Dolphin Within* programs, a two-day research and therapy sailing adventure for five people based on encounters with wild dolphins. Dolphins can facilitate human learning, alleviate depression, and help people with mental and physical disabilities, as shown by world research.

Measuring the "dolphin effect" on people is no small task, especially as we condemn and oppose research using captive dolphins. We are fortunate to live in Sydney, Australia near a bay where 80 bottlenose dolphins live in the wild all year. We have a research license that allows us to swim with the wild dolphins. Our tools are self-assessment questionnaires, drawings, photos and video films and an EEG biofeedback machine to monitor brain patterns.

First off, dolphins can help in dealing with phobias as shown by a Melbourne nurse named Prue. She was afraid of water but jumped in as soon as she saw the dolphins and wrote the following in her journal:

"I have always been terrified of interacting by myself in the sea. I am not familiar with it at all. So as soon as the dolphins arrived, the first night when we were all singing together, tears streamed from my eyes and I was overcome with emotion.

"The next morning I was alone, it was the first step, but I still didn't feel at ease. The dolphins were close; we jumped in. I didn't give it a second thought. I was in there interacting with them, listening to them chatting. It wasn't until the three of us were on the back of the dinghy that I thought, Oohh, what am I doing?

"Back on the boat, I read my pre-swim notes: 'My body had felt blocked, especially at the fingers, the energy could not break there.' Now I feel vital, alive like the sea, almost cleansed. The adrenaline and vitality and the work of conquering my fear of the ocean had exhausted me, and I felt into a tranquil sleep.

"Next step, diving, the fear of fears. Strange, I could have backed out but I didn't. Initially I was absolutely mortified. I clutched the hand of Jim, the dive instructor. Gradually, I relaxed into the restful ways of underwater, the beauty and the peace, the feeling of being at one. Jim's grip got lighter until our fingertips barely touched. I had done it. I had dived. The most incredible experience.

Upon our ascent, dolphins were very close, almost as if to say: 'Well done, Prue, we knew you could do it.' I had re-connected with myself. I've been a long time lost. I'm glad I found me. I feel mellow and at ease. I have found my Dolphin Within."

A week after the program, she passed her scuba diving certificate and has being diving regularly ever since.

Secondly, dolphins can help with dealing with emotions. Roger is blind and those who meet him see a strong personality. He challenges himself constantly. He does not see blindness as an issue.

On the yacht on the first day, we saw the usual, enthusiastic Roger who loves talking and joking. On the second day, another part of Roger, the "hidden part", came out. He started to cry in the afternoon, and he cried a lot at night. He went into the pain of becoming blind at the age of 14, his feeling of being isolated, "without a mate", as he said. The grief that he has never touched, expressed, or wanted to see was re-surfacing with the dolphin experience. After crying over two days, Roger was free to move on in his life without the weight of this grief.

Thirdly, dolphins can help in accessing hidden memories. Venus is a beautiful bush woman, who lives in the forest, and plays the didgeridoo. As soon as she was in the water with dolphins, she started crying. Back on the yacht she told me: "The dolphins put me back in contact with a childhood memory I had completely forgotten.

It is very painful. My stepfather was very cruel to me. I had a flashback to the day he tried to kill me."

Fourthly, dolphins can help in dealing with addictions. Daniel, a 14 year-old teenager, was in a very "dark space", as his mother described it to me when he came on the yacht with us. He was dressed in black, with black boots and a long dark raincoat. He had been drinking heavily, smoking a lot and taking drugs for the last year. During the dolphin weekend, Daniel discovered sailing, interacting with dolphins, scuba diving, and cooking for the whole team.

Back home, he said to his mum, "I'm giving up smoking; I'm a diver". He went to see the school psychologist and said, "I don't need your help any more; I'm okay now."

His results at school improved and a year later he had not smoked, drunk nor taken drugs. After a successful school year, he is doing a course to become a chef. His mother said joyfully, "I have a new son!"

Fifthly, dolphins can also help with tapping into creativity. Steve, a graphic designer, took part in the first program. Around the fire, he expressed his passion about sculpture. He brought the only piece of sculpture he had ever done, to show to the group. Following the program, he enrolled in a sculpture class to tap fully into his potential. Three years later he was expressing how sculpture had become the most important part in his life.

DOLPHINS

Ken, a well-known composer and musician, was improvising, singing and playing guitar on the yacht. Afterwards he said: "Since the weekend, I've been much more creative and am writing new songs. I've experienced a new creative flow." Ken composed a CD called "Dolphin Magic" to commemorate his *Dolphin Within* experience.

Now this is where art and science meet in a wonderful way. We got an electroencephalogram (EEG) machine to provide the means, through biofeedback, to show participants how to reproduce the state of consciousness that the dolphins' ultrasonic frequency puts them into. This has been very exciting for everyone.

Participants are tested at the beginning and end of the program. The assessment measures their capacity to reach different brain patterns. Our control group went through the same experience in terms of sailing and swimming, but did not have direct dolphin contact. Their brainwave patterns produce more alpha, which means that they are much more relaxed. Participants who have been through a dolphin encounter have shown three particular brainwave patterns.

First, Diane shows how the dolphins stimulated the production of theta waves. She came to us with a lot of emotional pain. After the trip she wrote: "I have many wonderful memories -- for a change. I can now truly say that I am happy for the most part. When I do get depressed, my thoughts return to the dolphin that swam close to me. The vision is very clear in my mind. I close my eyes and relive the experience. I feel more confident in my life. But mostly I feel relief to have lifted a heavy weight of pain from my heart."

Diane's brain pattern showed a significant increase in alpha and theta after the swim. She was unable to access the alpha and theta brainwaves before the swim. The dolphin experience gave her an experience of a new brain pattern. Her comments show that, months after the trip, she is still able to access this brain pattern any time she wants, when she needs it.

Secondly, Simon's experience provides a crossover example in brain waves. He is a very successful businessman who works a lot. He doesn't meditate or practice any relaxation techniques. He arrived on the yacht with one desire: to unwind.

Before his dolphin experience, Simon produced a lot of beta. When the brain cannot slow down and produce alpha and theta frequencies, individuals in the long term suffer from stress, anxiety and a lack of creativity.

Simon interacted with the dolphins on the first day of the trip. He could distinctly hear them underwater. Overnight, while dolphins came around the yacht, he dreamt of a dolphin taking him by the finger to swim with him. The experience was very moving and touching for him. On Sunday, he had another swim and then went on the brainwave (EEG) machine.

After the dolphin swim, Simon's brainwave pattern showed increased alpha, but what was even more remarkable was that Simon experienced an alpha-theta crossover, which means that the brain slows down even more and brings profound personality transformation by increasing warmth, abstract thinking, and stability. It decreases depression and anxiety, and can overcome addictions.

At the crossover point, the person experiences emotionally loaded even life-transforming moments -- creative insights, vivid memories from childhood, spiritual moments, and solutions to complex problems.

Kiran demonstrates a third brainwave pattern that results in having an awakened mind. Kiran is a young woman who has suffered from chronic fatigue syndrome for seven years. When she came on the yacht, it was the first time she had swum in the sea in four years. The dolphins were constantly next to her and they stayed an hour with her.

When we looked at her brain, we saw a rare configuration called "the awakened mind", one that combines four different wave patterns: beta (alertness, arousal and concentration), alpha (relaxation), theta (memory, integrative experiences and healing), and delta (profound rest and release of growth hormone).

Many who experience swimming with the dolphins have their lives transformed. Many participants change jobs and strike out in new and more satisfying directions. They are psychologically healthier, have more social poise, and are less stressed, less rigid, and less conforming. They have more self-acceptance and creativity and greater feelings of psychological well-being.

All this and more from swimming with the dolphins.

Dr. Olivia De Bergerac and William McDougall are co-founders of The Dolphin Society, an Australian non-profit research and educational foundation.

ξ CHAPTER FOUR ξ

DRAMATIC DREAMS

And yet, as angels in some brighter dreams
Call to the soul when man doth sleep,
So some strange thoughts transcend our wonted themes,
And into glory peep.
Henry Vaughan (1622 – 1695).

Why do we dream? No one really knows, but dream we do – about 2 hrs. each night, resulting in approximately 6 years of dreamtime in the average lifespan. Most people dream in colour with only slightly over 10% dreaming in black and white. Both Sigmund Freud and Carl Jung believed that dreams were an interactive process between the conscious and the unconscious minds.

People all over the world tend to dream of the same things -- being chased, flying, running slowly in place, falling, embarrassing moments, and teeth falling out among them. We are more apt to have dreams with negative emotions rather than positive ones, with anxiety being the most common.[xiii]

What do dreams mean? Where do they come from? There are

countless dream interpretation books with cleverly categorized headings that can easily be looked up. Nonetheless, often dreams tend to be puzzling because of the interplay of past, present, and future and the use of symbols and metaphors.

Surrealist painter Salvador Dali produced a piece of artwork in 1944 with the rather lengthy title of "Dream Caused by the Flight of a Bee around a Pomegranate a Second Before Awakening." Perhaps Dali knew that dreams often occur shortly before we wake up. The painting is also an indication of the relationship between the imaginative and the dream worlds.

Legend has it that Isaac Singer came up with the idea of how to thread a vertical sewing machine needle when he dreamt of a native tribe that inserted holes near the tips of their spears for the poison. Voila! A way to thread the needle. Coming up with a solution to a problem by "sleeping on it" can work. However, Singer probably never dreamt that his fifth wife, the beautiful French actress Isabella, would one day be the model for the famous Statue of Liberty.

Some dreams have a specific content that seems to come from the Other Side. They may contain a final goodbye to a loved one, a premonition or warning of some danger, or they may contain information re unfinished business.

Sometimes, however, as in the case of Mary, dreams are repeated over and over again until a particular desired action has taken place.

PROBABLY MARY

In a small prairie town in the late 1940's, everybody knew everybody else, and Jack and his girl were no exception. I can't remember her name any more but it was probably Mary. They had been childhood playmates and now, all grown up, they fell in love and got married. Jack was the second youngest in a large family so their wedding was a huge, happy affair, though Mary had few relatives herself.

Jack was an excellent musician, a violinist, and played at many weddings. After he got married however, he decided a regular income was more important than his love for music and he got an ordinary if boring 9-5 job in the hardware store. Mary also took on a job until their two children came along. Then she quit her job to stay home and look after the kids. Jack and Mary developed a loving and nurturing relationship that others envied.

After six years of a happy life together, Jack became desperately ill. Instead of getting better, he seemed to sink deeper and deeper into poor health. Finally the time came for him to say good-bye to his wife and kids.

Mary picked out Jack's best blue suit to bury her beloved husband in. The funeral was even bigger than the wedding had been. Mary was disconsolate.

After they buried him, Mary had to go back to work. But it wasn't long before she started having nightmares about her deceased husband. And they were always the same. In her dreams, Jack would repeatedly call to her, *"Mary, cover me up! I'm so cold. Please Mary, cover me up!"*

She had her shift changed to the night shift, so that she would finally be able to get some sleep, during the daytime hours. These dreams were beginning to affect her job and her relationship with her kids. But soon it was the same thing all over again.

"Mary, cover me up! I'm so cold. Please Mary, cover me up!"

It got so bad that she could neither sleep nor work. The town council was worried that she wouldn't be able to earn a living to support her two small children, so they stepped in to see what could be done to alleviate the problem.

"He's continually telling me to cover him up because he's cold," she told them.

The mayor asked if it would help if they unearthed the coffin so she could have a look. "Yes, she said reluctantly, "maybe that'll help."

So the town went to the cemetery and dug up the coffin. When they opened it, they found Jack's body totally naked. Someone had stolen the clothes he was to be buried in and left his nude body in the coffin.

They redressed the body in a new suit and another burial took place soon after.

All of Mary's nightmares vanished and she was able to resume her place in the work force.

PONTO BRONTE

I was Head Nurse in the Emergency Department and loved every minute of it. No day was like the last and unlikely to be anything like the next. The doctors and nurses reeked with youth and enthusiasm, eager to bring their unique skills to a tough job that was difficult by any standards.

Jacqueline, one of the staff nurses, was very sharp-witted and enjoyed putting me through my paces. She seldom accepted anything without questioning.

"Why can't this patient be transferred to the Intensive Care Unit now? We're in the middle of report just like they are!" or "The patient with the allergic reaction shouldn't be discharged yet. I don't care what the doctor says."

She was a good emergency room nurse. Everything had to have not only a logical reason, it had to have a very valid reason in her estimation. If something didn't make sense to her, I could hear the wheels churning and I teased her that black smoke poured out of her ears. She herself was fair-skinned, almost to the point of looking anaemic, a little chunky, her hair a white-blond. While I looked forward to the mental sparring and stimulation whenever she was on duty, she was not a close personal friend.

After one busy evening shift, I went home and crawled into bed. Immediately falling into a deep sleep, I dreamt about a car accident. The dream was unusually vivid in that I could clearly see the struts of a high level bridge from inside a car that seemed to be perched on a weird angle. There were other people around but the details became fuzzy. As I sleepily opened my eyes, I saw the green neon 2 A.M. on my clock radio, rolled over and went back to sleep.

When I awoke, the name "Ponto Bronte" was on my mind in a big way, playing over and over. Ponto Bronte. I remembered from high school French that the word "pont" meant "bridge" and so the phrase stuck in my mind. More so now that I had something in English to relate to, something I could understand.

At 3 P.M. I went in for the last shift of my stretch of seven evenings. There standing at the far end of the long desk of the nurses' station, was a wan-looking Jacqueline. The department was fairly quiet for a change and she and I did the usual narcotic count that was done at every shift change by one off-going nurse and one on-coming nurse.

"Demerol 75 mg…eleven, Demerol 100 mg…eighteen."

We signed the appropriate narcotics sheets and I waited for some question on either policy or procedure that I had come to expect from her. For once she had no questions or comments. She looked more ashen than usual, even by her pale standards, and remained silent.

"Jacqueline," I said, "I had the strangest dream last night. Something about a car accident on a high level bridge, at exactly 2 A.M. I know because I woke up and saw the time. And all I can remember are the words "Ponto Bronte. In other words the bridge at Bronte. Can you imagine me reverting to high school French for a dream translation?"

If I thought Jacqueline was ashen before, any hint of colour drained completely from her face as she stared at me.

"What did you say?"

"A dream I had. A car accident. At 2 A.M. Ponto Bronte. 'Bridge' in French. Get it?"

The strangest look crossed her face.

"Last night," she whispered, "I was in a car accident. At the bridge in Bronte. At 2 A.M."

"You're putting me on."

"I'm not!" she replied and I knew by the look on her face that she was for real.

"What happened? Were you hurt?"

"No. I'm okay. But my date lost control of the car and we veered off the highway. Rolled under the bridge. At one point, all I could see were the damn struts of the bridge."

This was precisely what I had seen in my dream, at exactly 2 A.M. But try as we might, neither of us could conjure up any possible explanation for my dream, why it had occurred, or what it meant.

There obviously was a lot of emotion for her during the accident, but why would I pick up on these events when I wasn't close to her, and what purpose could my "seeing" these events as they unfolded possibly have? If it was a premonition and I knew it was her, perhaps I could have warned her -- as if she would have believed me anyway. But what I dreamt was in real time.

In the days that followed, Jacqueline seldom questioned anything I asked her to do and more than once I caught her watching me with a strange look in her eye.

DECEMBER FOURTEENTH

I will always remember the fourteenth of December. It was the day I had this dream. That particular week I was on night shift at the hospital and when I came home in the morning I immediately fell asleep and began a vivid dream.

In the dream I traveled a great distance through many fog-like clouds, but it was not by any type of vehicle. It was just me. I was aware of a moving sensation and intense darkness. Finally, at the end of thick, thick clouds, I was able to make out the shape of a man. First I saw his body and although his head was there, I could not see his face.

I had become a child again. When the man offered his hand to me, I gladly took it and we walked through a tunnel of clouds, hand in hand. When I woke up I experienced an incredibly warm sensation and a deep feeling of peace.

In my own mind, I thought the dream meant that someone I knew was probably going to die. Right away I thought of a friend who lived in New York, hundreds of miles away. He had been diagnosed with cancer some time ago and because of the feeling of travelling and the great distances involved, I thought it must be him. That night at work I shared my dream and my fears with a co-worker.

On Tuesday, December twentieth, the phone rang. I was trying to get some rest before going in to work on the evening shift. My husband was at work and the kids were still in school. Twice I ignored the ringing of the phone, thinking that my rest was more important. When a third attempt was made to reach me, I decided to pick the phone up. It was my mom calling from Arizona with the terrible news that my dad had suffered a sudden cerebral hemorrhage.

After a horrible night amidst packing and trying to book a flight, I received continual updates from family members who were already in Arizona at the hospital. My brother called in the morning and said the situation had been very bad during the night and if anything, was deteriorating. I told him I had a flight booked and would arrive at 6:00 P.M. that evening to see my dad. I realized my dad might not be there when I arrived, so I asked my brother to kiss him for me and to tell him I loved him.

And so it was. They could not keep him alive. I never talked to my dear dad again and I never kissed him again because he died that day before I arrived.

I realized then that it was my father who had been in my dream, taking my hand as if I was a child, comforting me, knowing I would never hold his hand again. He had brought me a great distance to be with him because he knew I would not make it in time to see him.

I felt some small comfort in the thought that we had walked hand in hand one last time, that he did this for me.

HALT I SAY!

About twenty-five years ago, when I was in my early forties, I felt I really needed to know which of my parents would die first, in order to properly prepare for the future. Of course at the time, I didn't have a clue.

One night I was dreaming a perfectly ordinary dream. In this dream I was in a car with a friend of mine and we were driving along a country road. All of a sudden, right across the path of this car, my long-since deceased uncle, of whom I had been quite fond, appeared and held up his hand in front of the car, like a "HALT" sign!

He was dressed in a navy blue wool suit and striped red tie that I remembered him wearing when he was still alive. He stepped

HALT, I SAY!

right across my dream in such a significant way that I felt I could tell the difference between my dream and him really being there. He said two words to me: "Your mother." Then he vanished.

Sure enough, a few months later, Mother did die. In the interim, I was able to make arrangements that were beneficial to everyone in the family and I was grateful for my dream.

LETHAL WEAPON

Every time I saw my grandfather's old black car, it gave me the creeps. I had the feeling it should have been buried right along with him. But when the car was put up for sale with the rest of his estate, my brother Russ bought it. At twenty I was a year older than him, but he refused to listen to me when I tried to talk him out of buying this disturbing vehicle. Why should he listen to his sister when he really wanted this car?

I felt extremely uncomfortable with the car around and because both my brother and I were still living at home, I saw it all the time. For the next six months I would see him pull up in front of the house with that black monstrosity and every time I automatically thought of my dead grandfather. That car just gave me the creeps. There was something uncanny about it.

One Friday night I came home late and noticed that the car wasn't in the driveway or parked on the road as usual. "Man," I said to myself as I got ready for bed, "I wonder where that brother of mine is."

I fell into a deep sleep. I had a terrible dream that my brother was killed in a car accident. It was so real that I couldn't get over it. Some dreams you can forget about but this definitely wasn't one of them.

The next morning I asked my mom where Russ was because the car still wasn't home.

"He went up north to build a cottage with his buddy," she said. "I have no idea where he is."

"I had a dream last night that he was killed in a car accident," I said.

"Don't say things like that!"

"It was so real," I said. "I have to warn him to be careful driving home."

I called his girlfriend to see if she knew how I could get in touch with him but she had no idea. What made it even worse is that she too had a feeling that something bad was going to happen that weekend.

I went to work that day but I kept thinking about the dream. It played and replayed in my mind with no let-up. I couldn't forget it.

When my boyfriend came over after work I said, "We can't go out. I've got to get hold of Russ but I don't know where he is. I'd like to drive up north and try to find him."

Obviously this didn't make any sense at all. However I did everything I could to find him but it was impossible. Consequently, I was extremely upset the whole weekend. My brother was away, nobody knew where he was, and I couldn't forewarn him to drive carefully.

The weekend passed by uneventfully with no sign of Russ. On Monday morning my mom woke me up. She had a strange look on her face.

"Angie," she said, "Russ was in a car accident on his way home last night. He's okay but his car is totalled!"

Later that morning, Russ told us that the car ahead of him drove onto the soft shoulder of the road blowing lots of dust and gravel onto Russ' windshield. As a result, he lost control of the car and it rolled over and over before hurtling down an embankment. The car was smashed beyond recognition, a smoking heap three feet high. Unbelievably, Russ and his buddy walked away with a few minor scrapes.

If I hadn't talked about my dream all weekend prior to the accident, nobody would have ever believed me. It was a very perplexing experience.

DREAMS OF DEATH

Here are a couple weird experiences that are honest-to-God true. I woke up one morning from a dream, terrified. I could see my

Aunt grabbing her chest, crying that she was having a heart attack. When I related the dream to my husband, he told me to have a coffee and relax.

That evening while visiting my mother-in-law, my dad called to tell me that my aunt had just died of a heart attack. I was extremely upset. My husband and I talked about my dream and decided it was a freaky coincidence.

Four months later, I awoke from another disturbing dream involving the elderly lady across the hall from us in our apartment building. I told my husband I saw the paramedics entering her dimly lit apartment, and that I knew they were notifying the hospital about her death on her telephone. He again reassured me, telling me not to worry so much.

That evening, I went out to rent a movie, and when I returned, my husband gravely said, "Tell me right now exactly what you dreamt last night."

I asked him why, thinking he was kidding around.

"I'm not kidding," he said. "The paramedics pulled in seconds after you left. She's dead."

I was so bummed out. What does it all mean -- if anything? I personally have no idea.

DIRE WARNING

I know I changed after my dad died. My priorities changed. Things that used to be important to me were no longer important. I learned that people are important -- not things.

My dad was the first person who was close to me that I ever lost. When I was growing up, we weren't close because I was so rebellious, but later we shared a warm and loving relationship.

This year, three days before my dad's birthday in mid October, I had a very short dream in which he told me I was going to die.

I asked him what I was going to die from, and he told me it would be breast cancer.

I was quite upset. "How long have I got to live?" I asked.

"Four years or less," he replied.

That was it, the end of my dream.

They say the average age of dying from breast cancer is fifty or over. I'm forty-seven. I check my breasts regularly.

If this dream is true, he's warning me. I guess we'll all just have to wait and see, won't we.

ξ CHAPTER FIVE ξ

SHIPS AND SECRETS OF THE SEA

I remember …
the beauty and mystery of the ships,
And the magic of the sea.
Henry Wadsworth Longfellow (1807 - 1882)

I remember boarding a 50' sailboat on Lake Ontario with three friends one magical Sunday afternoon. The bright blue skies soon turned a dark slate colour, festooned with darker clouds. The strong winds that arose were surely from one of the four corners of the earth. Within moments we were totally drenched and breathless, knocked down onto the deck. We were tossed and turned in white-capped waves seemingly well beyond the capacity of our sailboat to withstand. The element of danger increased minute by minute and how we remained on the lake for another tumultuous fifty minutes, I honestly don't know, but it was one of the most enthralling and rivetting afternoons I have ever spent in my life.

Those who have made safe voyages over the years -- explorers, traders, leisure-seekers -- in whatever manner of boat or ship have done so only with the consent of Nature. Consider the sinking of the Titanic in April, 1912. It wasn't until 1985 that she was even found, in two separate pieces, some 12,600' underwater near the Grand Banks of Newfoundland. In the battle of Nature vs. technology, Nature always wins.

According to established maritime tradition, all ships are called "she", at least in the English language. (Russian ships are called "he.") And FYI, a boat can fit on a ship, but a ship can't fit on a boat.

The infamous ghost ship Mary Celeste, a 282-ton brigantine, was built in Nova Scotia, and was originally named the Amazon. Several unsettling events included the death of her first captain and a collision in the English Channel.

According to legend, Poseidon, the Greek god of the sea -- or Neptune, the Roman equivalent – has a record of the name of every vessel in the Ledger of the Deep. Consequently, re-naming ships is considered by sailors to be bad luck. Nonetheless, the Amazon was re-named the Mary Celeste.

In 1872 she was found under full sail in the Atlantic, totally deserted. None of the ten people on board were ever found. An expedition headed by adventure author Clive Cussler, of NUMA fame, discovered the ship off Haiti in 2001. In a subsequent fictionalized story, Sir Arthur Conan Doyle changed her name yet again, to Marie Celeste.

Strange things happen on ships.

THE TADOUSSAC

I worked in Collingwood, Canada for thirty years and I've been down south here for ten, so it's forty years in the shipbuilding business for me. Collingwood eventually closed in 1985 after over a hundred years of shipbuilding.

Way back then, we had trades workers that were very distinct such as welders, plumbers, and carpenters. In more modern times, it got to the point where there was a lot of demarcation between the trades and a welder would only weld, and a fitter would only fit.

Now they've amalgamated all the trades into one. Where there used to be five or six people each doing their own little thing, now one individual is expected to do everything. There are some who say this multi-tasking concept hasn't worked out exactly the way it was expected to in shipbuilding.

In 1959, we built a ship called the *TADOUSSAC.* It was a gigantic monster of a ship, some seven hundred and thirty feet. We were all very proud of her.

We had launched a good many ships, hundreds actually, and each had gone perfectly, exactly as planned. This particular day, there were about 250 people slaving away underneath the *TADOUSSAC*, myself included, working hard to prepare her for the launch. Suddenly, for no known reason, the ship slid sideways down the wooden ways and launched herself prematurely.

THE TADOUSSAC

Photo: Courtesy Don Coles - Great Lakes Aerial Photos

Forty people were seriously injured and two men (Douglas May and Alvin Wagner) were killed. These two were part of a group of twelve men that I was working with that day.

After that happened, a lot of people named the *TADOUSSAC* the *Devil Ship* because no satisfactory reason was ever found for the premature launching. We did have a number of small problems in building it but nothing you could put your finger on. But after the accident, people got to talking.

"This was a problem ship right from the start," they said.

I personally don't subscribe to anything supernatural but it nevertheless was an unusual occurrence in my own experience. After thirty-eight years, it's still on my mind. I carry a little poem that was written by one of the men who also was involved in the launching disaster. I admit I didn't think he could have written something so good. The poem is sort of crumpled up, difficult to make out. I've had it in my wallet ever since. Why? Damned if I know. It was published in our local paper up there.

AN ODE TO TWO GOOD MEN

In this little town of Collingwood
Nestled on Georgian Bay
A tragedy befell us
But why it happened who can say.

Shipbuilding is an industry
We are proud of in our town
And on the day we launch our ships
People come from miles around.

The year was 1959
A beautiful day in May
Staunch men had started at eight o'clock
To put another ship down the way.

With sledge-hammers the men begin
With two hundred strong,
Not knowing that in a little while
A terrible thing would go wrong.

There were ship-builders and welders
And tradesmen of every kind
Who fearlessly went underneath
With not a worry on their mind.

The ship is held by a trigger, blocks
But they proved of little use
For shortly after ten o'clock
An awful hell broke loose.

Someone shouted, "She's starting to move!
It was much sooner than the time
The men scrambled from underneath her
Through the mud, the dirt, and the grime.

It was a terrible nightmare
Only God knows the reason why
That two good men were carried beneath
The mighty ship to die.

The name of the ship was the TADOUSSAC
That was launched on that tragic day
But shipbuilders will always remember
Alvin Wagman and Douglas May.

by Russell Elliott

I know the ship is still out there sailing the lakes, because I see her on Lake Ontario on occasion. I don't know if it's true, but they tell me that since the *TADOUSSAC* has been sailing, other strange things have happened. Someone died in the engine room because of some bizarre accident and other peculiar things are continuing to happen.

Whether it's more than on other ships, I couldn't say.

THE ALEXANDER HENRY

The *ALEXANDER HENRY* was the first Canadian-built icebreaker for the Great Lakes. She was built at the Port Arthur Shipbuilding Co. and launched in 1958.

In the early sixties, the ship was stationed out of the Canadian Coast Guard base in Parry Sound. The captain was a man who lived for his work and he loved that ship passionately. His home was at the end of the road near the dock, and he always used to come down with his dog, Frazzles. The ship was a home away from home for both of them. I sailed briefly with this captain, went to another ship, and when I came back he had already died.

After the captain's death, Frazzles pined for his master. He used to sit on the dock waiting for the ship to come in, come aboard and go straight to the captain's cabin. That was spooky enough but for the next ten years, there were strange goings-on aboard that ship.

I heard strange sounds on numerous occasions when the ship was in. Once there were a few people on board but we all knew with certainty that nobody was in the cabin. I was sitting in the Officers' Lounge, which was directly underneath the cabin, and I heard water running and footsteps walking around in the area of the cabin. Nobody was in there and the door was locked.

One weekend one of the stewardesses, Elaine, asked me to unlock the door to the captain's cabin so she could get it made up. I

THE ALEXANDER HENRY

Photo: Courtesy Marine Museum of the Great Lakes, Kingston, Ont.

carried the keys for security reasons. I unlocked it for her, and she said, "Okay, I'll go in and make it up as soon as I have a chance."

Elaine was known and admired as a no-nonsense kind of lady, afraid of nothing and nobody. She was her own person in every sense of the word.

An hour later, I heard a blood-curdling scream coming from the captain's cabin. I darted down there to find Elaine standing in the middle of the room, her face contorted and frightened.

"What's wrong?"

"I can feel somebody in here, a presence," she whispered whirling around. "I know there's somebody in here."

I looked around. The cabin was empty but it was very cold.

The next weekend, Elaine made the bed and tidied up the cabin. The following day, she went in for one final check. She discovered that the bedclothes were indented as if someone had been lying on the bed and there was an imprint of a head on the pillow. Again the door had been locked. There was no way for these things to happen normally.

She did not like the idea of having to do that cabin up when the captain would be gone for the weekend and it would be empty. Other Commanding Officers would be on then. Because these odd occurrences really bothered her, she said, "Cap, can I do your room up today before you go for the weekend?" He said okay and the room was locked up afterwards as usual.

On Monday, the captain called her up to explain the state of the cabin. There were papers all over the desk and the coffee table. The bed looked like somebody had been lying on it. It wasn't messed up, but the imprint of a body was on the bed. There's absolutely no way anyone as conscientious as Elaine would ever have left the cabin like that.

Finally, one weekend that I was on duty, Elaine sought me out. Her face was white as a sheet. "I'm never going in there again!" she declared.

"Why?" I asked.

"Either there's somebody in there or someone's playing a joke on me. Either way, I don't like it."

"You know nobody's allowed in those cabins, Elaine," I said. "This is no prank. Let's go and check it out right now."

We went in and everything seemed to be in order, except for one thing. It was so freezing cold in there that it felt like the air conditioning had been turned on full force. The only catch was, the ship never had air conditioning. Pretty weird.

I think were it not for Elaine, some might have treated these incidents as pranks, but her sterling character gave credibility to these outlandish events. As a result, it wasn't something that was treated lightly or joked about. It was serious and was discussed at the mess table after every weekend.

"How was the weekend? Quiet? Did the old man come down?"

Everyone knew what was being referred to. And some weekends there wouldn't be a peep. There's absolutely no explanation and I honestly felt at that point that the captain really was coming down to his cabin. The strange thing is that most of this stuff would be going on when Frazzles was sitting on the dock, pining away for his lost master.

We never could find anything. A lot of people thought that the ship was haunted, that the captain had never left. The visitations in the cabin pretty well stopped when the dog quit coming. We soon learned that Frazzles had died. But even after the death of the dog, the watchman still heard footsteps on the grating of the bridge when no one was there.

Myself, I'm an engineer. I could always tell if somebody was approaching the engine room because their feet would rattle the deck plates and the density of their body would muffle the noise that came from the generating compartment where machinery was running.

But bizarre things happened when I was on watch. I heard the deck plates rattling as if someone was walking there, but there wasn't any change in the sounds from the engine room. It was like a mass was making noise on the deck plates but wasn't solid enough to muffle the noise.

Or the opposite would be true. The noise would be muffled but the deck plates were silent. This happened so many times that I had to get out of the engine room because my head was spinning. It just didn't make any sense.

This was long after the visitations to the cabin had quit. Maybe it was just wild imagination but at least nobody was ever harmed. For many years I thought it was a couple of real clever watchmen that were trying to do a number on us but it happened to too many people, too many times. Finally we put it down to the old man's spirit. Whether he was making rounds or looking for something, I have no idea.

The *ALEXANDER HENRY* is now retired as a museum and is a bed and breakfast in Kingston.[xiv] I know his cabin has been opened up, but whether there have been any strange sightings or not, I haven't heard."

UUO - UNIDENTIFIED UNDERWATER OBJECT ©

Back in the 1970's, a couple of weeks before cyclone *Tracy* hit Darwin, Australia on Christmas Eve, I was on the 12-4 watch on the bridge of a small cargo ship, the *M.V. NYANDA*, some eighty miles out of Darwin and heading for port. It was about 1:00 A.M. and there was only the Third Mate and myself on the bridge.

We saw a massive UFO enter the atmosphere and land in the ocean a few miles off the port quarter. It was so close we could see every detail and texture on its surface. We picked it up on the radar briefly and it looked to be about half-a-mile long. It looked like a huge lump of glowing rock, but was much too even to be natural. It was roughly oval shaped, covered with large round pockmarks, and had a glowing bright blue-green halo around it. It had no tail such as a meteor would have and it landed slowly and gently, with no noticeable splash.

The sea glowed eerily over a very large area after it was submerged and we could see it glowing behind us for some time after we'd left the area. The Third Mate, not wanting to be laughed at, suggested we keep this to ourselves.

At dawn the next morning, while tying the ship up, I looked out to sea and saw another big one come down far out to sea, identical to the first. It landed in roughly the same area as the first one had.

A few years later, while talking about this to another shipmate, Shannon, he claimed to have had a similar experience around about the same time, within a hundred miles of the area that I had seen the huge blue-green ship/thing land. He was on a survey ship, which is a small ship with a fifteen-man crew. The watch sighted a blue-green glow coming from the ocean surface a few miles away and the skipper ordered a change of course to check it out.

When they got to the glowing area, they found the sea was lit up by an eerie green light for a couple of miles in all directions. The light was coming from deep in the ocean. It was almost as bright as day, according to Shannon, but green. All the crew came up on deck to see it. Using their sophisticated sonar set-up, they found a very large object on the ocean floor that they estimated to be more than a mile long. That's bloody huge, mate! As they began taking their first readings the thing moved away rapidly, and then stopped again a few miles away. The ship again followed it and took more sonar readings.

This time the Unidentified Underwater Object (UUO) took off and it moved directly underneath the ship. It took some time to move completely past them due to its sheer size and length. It then picked up speed quickly and vanished in several seconds, speeding away far out to sea at an impossible speed. The whole crew watched the blue-green halo of light as it headed for the horizon. None of them said a word about it and this episode, like many others I have heard like it, has never been properly reported. This all happened in roughly the same area, about eighty miles off the coast of Darwin.

On Christmas Eve, a couple of weeks after I saw the big ship/thing land, cyclone *Tracy* struck Darwin and totally blew it away. My ship was there the day after the cyclone hit, (Boxing Day), having weathered the storm out at sea. Actually, running for our bloody lives is more like it. We started pulling bodies out of the water with grappling hooks as soon as we hit the bay. They were fishermen mostly, killed trying to save their boats.

The whole ship was stunned into absolute silence as we made our way at DEAD SLOW towards the wharf. I was standing by the winch controls in the bow and looked over at my boson, Tommy, and watched a single tear roll down his hard weathered face. He pulled a flask of rum from his shirt and took a long swig, then handed it to me. The rum helped some.

We had a hell of a job tying up to the wharf. It was totally trashed. All the cranes were smashed up and metal beams and timber and wires and busted sea containers were hanging over the sides every which way. We sat dead in the water until the skipper worked out a way to tie us up. Eventually, we sent a lifeboat over with some men to man the wharf and clear some of the debris away. We used a rocket gun to get a line ashore. We could have thrown heaving lines, but the skipper had always wanted to try out the new rocket gun.

If not for our skipper having a funny feeling and heading out to sea instead of heading directly to Darwin, we'd have gone down with all hands, that's for bloody sure. The weather reports all said *Tracy* had completely missed Darwin, right up until just before she suddenly changed direction and slammed back into Darwin with a vengeance. Most people were asleep, and there was no way of getting hold of everyone. There's nothing afloat that could have withstood the 200 mph+ winds and seas like falling high-rises that *Tracy* whipped up. No one really knows how high the wind speed got, as the local weather station got blown away. They recovered a wind speed indicator from it later. The needle was broken and stuck well past its limit of 160 mph.

Many of my shipmates had cursed the skipper that night (God bless his cotton socks) and said he was a paranoid bastard for taking us that far out to sea at full speed into the swell. No sailor likes heading "into" a heavy swell. The ship moves strangely and even old hands get seasick (funny that). They all wanted to get ashore fast and hit the pubs and the local girls.

I was standing in the middle of downtown Darwin a few days after *Tracy* hit. It was so eerie and quiet. I could hear the sound of a small child sobbing somewhere nearby, and the sombre sounds of men searching through wreckage, the sliding of rubble and timber and the clinking and crunching of broken glass. All the traffic lights and steel street light poles were bent flat to the ground. Looking around the Darwin suburbs reminded me of some pictures I'd seen of Hiroshima after the A-bomb was dropped. There was nothing standing above waist high, just a huge mass of rubble as far as I could see.

Behind me, along the main street, a few of the larger buildings still stood, after a fashion. The hospital was a sturdy, four-story, double brick building. You'd think you'd be safe in there, but it had one entire wall blown out and the roof torn completely off. It looked like a broken doll's house from a distance.

Along the main street were several fishing boats and small ships, tugboats and such, blown there by the storm. This added a really weird and unreal touch to the whole scene. Everything was out of place and upside down and it seemed almost obscene to have a 100-ton ocean-going tug nosed up into the local pub.

Most of the people we met were very, very quiet, with a sort of vacant look in their eyes, while others cried all the time. Some of us cried with them and tried to comfort them as best we could. There was a heavy atmosphere of shock and pain over the town, like the kind you get at an auto wreck where someone has just died violently. It puts shivers up my spine just thinking about it.

I saw a group of young soldiers crying hysterically. They had just found a little girl shut in an old refrigerator. They hadn't found her in time and she had asphyxiated. We guessed her parents must have put her in there when their house started breaking up. Her parents were never found. Most people survived out in the open, by hiding behind their front steps and other heavy low structures, out of the killing wind. Most of those who stayed in their homes died and were never found.

The devastation left by *Tracy* became a political issue, and for some reason the authorities decided a high death toll would make them look bad -- what with an election just around the corner! Because Darwin is tropical and Australian, i.e. very hot and humid, the standard garb there is shorts and thongs.

To be an official 'dead person' you had to be found fairly intact with ID on your person, or else have someone clearly identify you. The official death toll was about forty-five, but many more than that were actually killed. They dug a lot of graves with bulldozers, piled all the broken bodies and bits and pieces into the holes, covered them with lime and then filled them in again. Further out of town, entire aboriginal settlements were wiped out, never to be seen again.

We helped all we could and stayed an extra week till other ships and the army got there. The emergency crews plugged the town into our ship's generators and for a few days we acted as the power station. The power station had got blown away. We unloaded everything we had on board, even stuff headed for other ports, using our own cranes and derricks. The wharf gear was totally trashed. We drank a lot on the way back to Fremantle, but it was a quiet trip for all that.

A couple of months later, I visited one part of the rain forest, several miles out of town. It was an amazing sight. Ancient forests had been smashed to the ground, just so much kindling to cyclone *Tracy*. We had planned to go fishing but it was totally impassable, even on foot. All the trees had been blown over and were stacked, messily, twenty or thirty feet high.

A few months later, a man (I forget his name) wrote and released a poignant ballad about cyclone *Tracy*. It goes something like this: "Santa never made it to Darwin… a big wind came and blew the town away… "

The song still brings a tear to my eye when I hear it on the radio. *Robert Bruce, mystic & author, Australia*

CANADIAN COAST GUARD CRAMPS

I was stationed in Thunder Bay on a Canadian Coast Guard ship when I had an experience I will never forget.

My wife was in Midland expecting our first child and I had arranged to have some time off to be with her for the birth. Two weeks before her due date, it was late at night and I was having such terrible stomach cramps and pains that they woke me up. I knew it wasn't something I had eaten, it was just something I had to suffer through. Then, despite the horrible cramping, and I don't know how I can explain it, but I got up and got dressed. I *knew* I would have to answer the phone. It certainly wasn't because I heard the phone ring, because it was kept at the other end of the ship and I couldn't possibly know if it was ringing. But I just *knew*. Within minutes, the watchman came and knocked on the door.

"Cli-iff, pho-one. It's ho-ome."

When I got to the phone a neighbour said, "We took your wife to the hospital, her labour pains have already started." With that, all of *my* pains disappeared as suddenly as they had started. I went back to bed.

At that time, for security reasons, the watchman always took the phone and locked it up in the box so nobody could access it. And this particular night it rang and rang and rang. It would quit and then it would ring again.

It was ringing so much that one of the deck officers said to the captain, "Captain, something's up because the phone won't stop ringing."

Finally they unlocked the box and answered the phone. It was for me.

The ship was tied up but by the time I made arrangements to get to the airport and over to the hospital, my little daughter had made her appearance. She arrived about an hour after I got the call. She was two weeks early.

There was a second incident. My wife is intuitive as heck. In 1990 I was working on a ship called the *BARTLETT* when I had a heart attack. My wife knew something was wrong and she was actually making preparations with the kids without being forewarned. When the phone call came she was all ready. She knew about it from the time I was hospitalized until a nurse phoned her.

She gets a mental picture of events before they happen. Even now, she and I will be watching TV and she'll say that our daughter is going to call. Within minutes, the phone rings and it's our daughter.

My wife has always been that way, very perceptive to everything that's going on around her. She picks up vibrations and auras of other people. She says I'm a better judge of character than she is, but I just get a feeling or vibes from people and I either like them or I don't. Even my kids say, "Dad, you've never been wrong yet."

Everybody says my wife and I are so perfectly matched. We were born nine months apart; I'm the older. Each of us knows what the other is thinking, like with the labour pains. She knows when I'm in trouble and I know when she's in trouble. It's a nice feeling except for the fact that I can't get away with anything.

LIGHTHOUSE-KEEPER'S CALL

In my line of work, I get involved in pretty dangerous rescue situations. Last fall a 115-foot American passenger cruiser sank. The boat had drifted loose after the propellers had been taken off. Fortunately, only the owner and the mate were on board at the time. We were in a horrendous storm with 70-80 knot winds. Even though we were less than fifteen miles from land, we were unable to get back for three days because the weather was so unbelievably wild with the lowest barometric pressure ever recorded in that area.

When daylight finally came the next day, looking out to seaward, there were hundreds of white water spouts or mini-tornadoes up to about fifty feet high. It was like watching ballerinas skip across the water. We were able to rescue the two men on board and the cruiser was taken in tow by a 1,000 ft. tanker. A whole series of events led to its eventual demise.

The odd thing is that something strange happened in that same area some fifteen years ago. I was given a call by the head lighthouse-keeper at Angus Island.

He reported that there was a spaceship hovering just off the island, second water out of Lake Superior. The Rescue Coordination Centre (RCC) suggested we respond immediately.

"You better go check it out," the RCC said. "Maybe something is going on out there."

The island is about seventeen miles from the base. We didn't know what we were going to do if we saw the UFO, but we went anyway. On the way out there, we were in contact with the light-keeper and while we were still en route, he told us that it took us so long to get there, that the spaceship had already gone.

I spoke with the light-keeper and believe me, they're a breed unto themselves. He swore up and down that he saw a green light coming and that this *thing* hovered and pointed down at the water while he made several phone calls.

Some years later, this lighthouse keeper died in his lighthouse and we ended up bringing him back to the mainland. He was a young man too, under fifty.

I've never seen any UFOs or anything like that, aside from the shooting stars that we can see on a nice clear night. That was the weirdest thing I ever came up against, that we were actually responding to a UFO call. There was no explanation that I ever heard.

CURRENTLY NO WIND

The *MONTMORENCY* wasn't made for icebreaking, but

nonetheless the Canadian Coast Guard used this ship as a very light icebreaker, re-supplying lighthouses, doing the navigational aids and buoy tender.

This happened one October evening on the 4–8 watch. We were on our way back up to Parry Sound from Kingston dry-dock. To be precise, we were in the middle of the lake, SSW of Point Petrie or the southern tip of Prince Edward County.

When there has been no wind and suddenly the wind rises up and comes at you across the lake, it looks like a rainstorm. Judging by the head on the water now, it looked like there was a swell approaching.

"This is interesting," I said to the captain, "it looks like we have a squall coming our way."

In fact, on the side we were approaching from, the water was calm. When we went into it, there was still no wind but there was a sideways movement of an enormous amount of water. It was like a great up-welling of water, and I mean *a great* up-welling of water, probably the equivalent of going into the Gulf Stream.

Based on the twenty-four to twenty-six foot width of the ship, this current moved us sideways about thirty feet with no problem at all. It was the current with no wind at all. Caused by what, I have no idea.

We eventually got out of it. The ship was 169 feet, so this would have involved between three-quarters to a mile on each side of us that was noticeable, and about two hundred to three hundred feet wide.

I've run across something like this before on the tip of Long Point and the tip of the Bruce Peninsula. These places are areas where the currents will set up with wind shifts or strong winds of moderate to strong velocities for a continuous period of time. But when this happened, we were in the middle of the lake with *no* wind.

I have no idea how this happened or what caused it. Strange, is all I can say.

RADAR SCREEN BLIP

It was late August on the *ALEXANDER HENRY,* the Canadian Coast Guard ship that had come out in '59. We had been doing a re-supply trip to the lake stations on Lake Superior and now were looking forward to getting in to our base at Parry Sound.

It was the sort of warm, hazy night where, out on the water, you couldn't tell whether the visibility was ten miles or one mile. We were down-bound on Lake Huron coming from detour to Cove Island and I was on the midnight to four A.M. watch as wheelsman.

We were maybe twelve to fifteen miles SE from Great Duck Island when a target appeared on the radar screen, nine miles directly ahead of us. It kept coming closer and closer. As it came to within three to four miles of us, we altered course to avoid collision.

It changed its position as well until it was coming ahead of us again. It continued to come in closer. The mate that was on watch said, "Ooh, this is strange, this isn't quite right" and he got the captain up to the bridge to look at it.

We kept watching and watching and I can't just think exactly what course we were steering but eventually he went through ninety degrees of course change and had almost stopped the ship. We were down to DEAD SLOW in speed till the target was only about a mile to three-quarters of a mile away and then it disappeared off the radar screen. All initial indications were that it was a ship and so we came back on to our original course, back up to full speed.

Within three minutes this thing was back again. Only, this time, we went in a full circle trying to avoid it. By this time, we were very apprehensive. Again, when we altered course, it moved directly ahead of us, kept moving in closer, and then disappeared off the radar screen, only to reappear again. This happened three times between one A.M. and two A.M.

What did I think it was? A UFO, something unexplained, is all I can say. We were between fifteen and twenty miles off land, bearing in mind that this was mid to late August on a night when the visibility was definitely less than fifteen miles.

Entries about this incident were made into the log and into the weekly report. At the time I was only the wheelsman, and as far as I know, nothing ever came of these reports.

However, it goes one step further. At four A.M. at the end of the watch, I went into the Crew's Mess. The oiler who works in the engine room had just gotten off watch too. He was the type of guy who was very talkative, always telling jokes. This morning however, he had a very solemn air about him.

"Hi," I said. "How are you doing?"

"Oh fine. Not too bad."

Just general talking, but while we were going through this, he definitely wasn't his usual self.

"I noticed we were making some course alterations. Is there something strange going on?" he asked.

"Well, yeah, there was. Why?"

"Well, I don't know if I should tell anybody," he said with a worried look on his face. "I don't know what it was. But yeah, something bothered me and I'm going to tell you."

He went on to explain. "You know how when you get to know people, you look at them from the back and you know who it is, even from a distance."

"Yes," I said.

"This being the case, especially here on the ship, where the people are there for a given length of time, when you see somebody walking down a corridor or a hallway, you know who it is. You say, 'There's so-and-so, he's going to the head' or 'He's going to the mess' or whatever."

"What's your point?" I asked wearily. It had been a long night.

For all intents and purposes, the *ALEXANDER HENRY* was two decks high. He explained that about the same time that all the course changes were being made, he was down in the engine room, on the lower part.

Looking aft, to your left-hand side, there would be the doorway to the engine room and he had been doing something in the forward part in the engine room and just happened to glance up. There's a set of stairs going up to a grated landing and you could either go to the engine room exit or if you went straight back, you would go into the generator room.

As he looked up, he saw somebody who had just turned left and went into the generator room. What struck him was, he didn't know who it was. He couldn't recognize him. He went through the generator room searching for this person with a fine-tooth comb, but couldn't find anyone there.

He knew all thirty-one people on board but he didn't recognize this person who had disappeared into the generator room. To say he was worried would be a gross understatement. He'd thought he'd seen a ghost because in fact, the *ALEXANDER HENRY* had a reputation for being haunted. It was as simple as that.

When I was a kid, I remember my father and other older people saying that this particular skipper (captain) had said in a joking sort of way, that because of the changes in management and administration, that when he quit sailing and finally died, that he was going to come back and haunt them.

As it happened, due to ill health, probably brought on by changes and stress, he did in fact pass away while still a relatively young man.

Later, everyone accepted that the *ALEXANDER HENRY* was haunted because this certain skipper really did come back.

ξ CHAPTER SIX ξ

CHARISMATIC KIDS

Phone for the fish-knives, Norman,
As Cook is a little unnverved;
You kiddies have crumpled the serviettes
And I must have things daintily served.
Sir John Betjeman (1906 – 1984)

Much has recently been made of kids who apparently are more psychic and more enlightened than their predecessors. They have been called by various names like the Indigo children, Rainbow, Crystal, Star, or Super Psychic kids. Some are said to be able to move objects through the air at will by using their minds or accomplish even stranger feats like seeing with their hands and feet.

Some of these super kids are able to show that whatever they think actually becomes their reality. In Rhonda Byrne's movie "The Secret," many well-known people (adults) are depicted as having reached their goals, whether financial, material, career, or relationship-related by the process of focussed, selective and repetitive visualization. The point is also made that, whether we are aware of it or not, each of us is making our own reality by our thoughts even without our conscious awareness of the process.

Perhaps one of the most endearing traits of almost all kids though, has always been their trusting natures and the gift of accepting what is before them with open-eyed innocence.

Awareness. Openness. Acceptance. No questions asked.

Take for instance, the case of little Ronnie in the story that follows.

GUARDIAN ANGEL

My husband and I were perfectly happy with our loving family of two daughters and one son. Then suddenly in February of 1993 our four-year-old son Ronnie, the youngest, was diagnosed with acute myeloid leukemia, a rare and often fatal form of childhood cancer.

We had many fears knowing that Ronnie faced difficult chemotherapy for up to a year and then possibly the ordeal of a bone marrow transplant.

Then, in April, Ronnie told us something strange. "God was in my dream," he said casually.

"What do you mean God was in your dream? What was He doing?" I asked.

"He was talking to me and we sat and watched the angels singing."

"What did God say?"

"Oh, we were just talking."

"Who else was there?"

"Jesus was there."

"Oh okay! What did God look like?

"He was bright. He was very bright with lots of light behind Him."

"Was He big? Was He small? Describe Him like daddy or somebody else you know."

"He was big like Daddy."

"What was Jesus like?"

"He was small like me and God was hugging him because He loves him."

This was my four-year-old talking and I was absolutely floored. I was desperately trying not to lead him into thinking anything. I wanted everything to come only from what he said.

I asked again what God looked like.

"You know Mommy, God and Jesus look exactly the same, but they're different."

Here's a four-year-old trying to explain the trilogy.

"What do you mean, 'They look exactly the same but they're different'?"

"They look exactly the same but they're different. I can't tell you how they're different."

"Okay. Did God tell you anything that you remember?"

"That He was going to make me better."

Ohhhh! Okay! This is good!

At this point, Ronnie was at home but he had already started the chemotherapy. I know it was at a time when we had very mixed feelings of whether or not we should go through with the bone marrow transplant. The reason we had mixed feelings is that when the doctors originally told us his diagnosis, they said he could go through conventional chemotherapy for a year. Then we would go through with the bone marrow transplant only if he had a relapse because it was such a risky procedure.

Now all of a sudden, three months into the chemotherapy, the doctors said, "His older sister Jennifer is a match, let's go with the transplant."

"Now hold it. Wait a minute! Originally, you told us it would be chemotherapy for a year and then, if he relapses, to go with the transplant."

And so we had very mixed feelings. We were afraid. We'd have him for a year if we went with the chemo, but if he didn't survive the transplant, we'd only have him a couple of months. It was a very difficult decision to make.

I went to McMaster University and researched in the library for about three hours, doing all this reading on bone marrow transplants. We had another discussion with the doctor. My husband and I said, "If only someone could give us an answer."

When Ronnie told us his dream, we decided to go ahead with the transplant. I put a lot of faith into what Ronnie told us but he didn't know that's why we actually went ahead with the bone marrow transplant. I really felt this was our answer. I said to my husband, "God gave us Jennifer, and she's as close to a one hundred percent match as we're going to get from what the doctors told us." I felt good about our decision.

Ronnie went through three weeks of heavy chemotherapy to get into remission. Actually he was in remission after the second week and then he had the third week to make sure they had knocked it out good. That was in April. Once his blood counts came up, the doctors said okay to the bone marrow. This was in May of '93.

When he went in he had all these tests like an echocardiogram and blood work. The second day they did a bone marrow aspiration to make sure he was still in remission and a spinal tap because nothing had shown in the spinal fluid up to that point.

When they did the spinal tap they also gave him his first injection of chemo into his spinal fluid. This happened at 9 AM and he was sedated for that. He had some hallucinations and had the doctors laughing, telling them that their eyes were dancing and that he was flying around the room.

After the sedation wore off, he had his breakfast then fell asleep. When he woke up, he enjoyed his lunch. Then we were having a regular day. We played and he visited with his sisters in the afternoon out in the visiting area because they weren't allowed on the isolation ward.

After supper we played different games and at eight o'clock that night, we were playing his favourite game of cards, Crazy Eight's. I was sitting at the foot of his bed and he was up at the head.

That's when he looked over my shoulder and said, "Mommy, there's an angel behind you."

I said, "What do you mean, there's an angel behind me?"

His face was tranquil and relaxed. He was watching over top of me, and behind. I could tell he was watching something. We had never specifically talked about angels. We went to church and talked about God and Jesus a bit, but angels weren't a big discussion in our home. We're not pushy that way.

So when he told me about this angel, I thought, Oh no, God changed His mind, maybe this angel came to prepare Ronnie to come!

"Well what does she look like?" I asked.

"She's glowing. She's got this white, white light coming from her. She's beautiful. She's got long hair like yours."

He was swaying slightly. "She's kind of floating there."

ANGEL

I could see him watching her over my shoulder. I tried to peek but I didn't want to scare her away. I was positive she was there. There was no doubt in my mind. According to him, she had white wings that came out from behind her, a white glowing dress with a bright gold light shining from the area of her chest.

"What's her name?" I asked him.

All of a sudden he got really shy and he put his head down. "I dunno," he whispered.

"Well ask her."

"No, Mommy, I'm not gonna' ask her. You ask her."

"Ronnie, I can't see her. You're going to have to ask her."

"No, I can't ask her. You ask her."

"Ronnie, you're going to have to ask her because I can't see her."

He got this little grin and looked over my shoulder. "What's your name?"

He was looking, waiting for an answer. Then he got this *huge* grin on his face and his eyes were sparkling. "It's Wendy, Mommy," he giggled.

"Why is Wendy here?"

"I dunno."

"Well, ask her."

Again he started the whole thing. "I'm not gonna' ask her, you ask her."

"Ronnie, I didn't hear her tell you her name. I can't hear her. I can't see her. You're going to have to ask her."

"I don't wanna' ask her."

"Oh *please* ask her… why is she here?"

A pause. Then, "Why are you here?"

You can tell when a child is listening. His whole face is looking and his eyes are looking.

Picture this. He had a double lumen catheter with about four different IV tubes connected to him. He crawled over to me, across the cards, and whispered in my ear in a singsong voice, "To keep an eye on me." The he started giggling like crazy.

"To keep an eye on you, this is good," I said.

I was afraid to ask any more questions but since we seemed to have a direct line, I decided to go for it. "Ronnie," I said gently, "ask her if you're going to get better."

Just then Jane, one of the nurses, came in.

"Jane," I snapped. "Hurry up!"

Quickly I told her what happened.

"I don't doubt it," she replied. "We've had kids say things like this before. This is probably real."

Wendy would have been right behind the door when Jane came in, still in Ronnie's line of sight.

"Is Wendy still here?" I asked Ronnie tentatively.

"No, she's gone," he muttered, like it was no big deal. Then looking around he said, "Oh there she is! By the chair. She's watching to see if Jane does a good job."

Naturally, Jane heard all this. Smiling, she said, "Okay. I'm being very careful." She checked all his IV lines and on her way out asked me to let her know what Wendy's answer was. I nodded in assent.

Alone again, I said, "Ronnie, ask her."

"Mommy, I'm not going to ask her."

"Just ask her if you're going to get better."

He looked towards the window where the chair was.

"Am I going to get better?"

Then he turned to me with this matter-of-fact look and he said,

"Mommy, I already told you God and the other angels said I was going to get better. You don't have to ask anymore!"

I could not believe this answer from my four-year-old. With relief in my heart, I said, "Thank you, Wendy."

We had been told that twenty-one days in isolation was the average and we were marking them off as we went. We were now on day fifteen.

Ronnie wanted to be home for Father's Day but the doctors took me aside and said, "Don't get his hopes up. Chances are he might get an infection and will have to do the ten-day protocol with antibiotics."

But Ronnie insisted all along that he would be home for Father's Day and he ended up having one of the fastest recoveries the doctors had ever seen. We gratefully took him home the Monday before Father's Day, much to the delight of my husband and two daughters.

Ronnie recovered fully.

When Christmas came, we all went to my aunt's house. Following a delicious turkey dinner, I asked the kids to go to the bedroom for a rest period.

A couple of days later, my husband and I were tucking Ronnie into bed. I asked Ronnie if he had ever seen Wendy again.

"Yeah," he said.

"When?"

"Remember when you told us we had to rest at that aunt's house? In the bedroom?"

"Wendy came then?"

"Yeah."

"What did she do?"

"She came with other angels."

"How many other angels?"

He looked up at the ceiling as if he were recalling what he had seen and counted on his fingers.

"Ten," he said at last. "There were ten other angels."

"What were they doing?"

"They were singing to me."

Always paranoid, I asked why Wendy had come.

"She said she was just checking on me."

With that he turned over and fell into a peaceful sleep. My husband and I beamed.

The next year, just before Halloween, Ronnie asked me what the devil looked like.

"I don't know," I said. "Some people have ideas of what he looks like, with a long red cape and red horns. Some like to dress up like the devil for Halloween."

"Why don't people dress up like God?" he demanded.

"Because nobody knows what God looks like."

"That's easy," Ronnie said with conviction. "All you have to do is put on a white gown that moves softly and stand in front of big bright lights with rainbow colours all through them. Then you'll look like God!"

What could I say? I was floored.

One Sunday, quite some time later, we were in church for the four o'clock mass because we had missed the morning one. We were sitting quite near the front and Ronnie kept looking over his left shoulder.

"Ronnie, what are you doing?" I demanded.

"Looking at Wendy," he replied in a loud whisper.

I looked back. “What do you mean, ‘Looking at Wendy.’ Where is she?”

“She’s sitting back there. Can’t you see her? Can’t you see her Mommy?” and he pointed to the back, close to the organist.

“I can’t see her.”

“She’s right there!”

“What is she doing?”

“She’s going like this,” and he used the hand motion to indicate TURN AROUND. I couldn’t help but laugh out loud in church.

Yet another time, Ronnie said that Wendy was in one of his dreams. He said he was playing with his friends in the dream, looked up into the sky and saw God, Wendy, and some other angels who were singing. He felt that Wendy was keeping an eye on him.

I truly believe that Ronnie has had divine intervention. I’m one hundred percent sure of this. He’s been given a second chance for some reason and I believe there’s a special purpose for him. I don’t know what it is, it’ll come out as he grows up. Maybe his story will touch somebody in a way that will help them, I don’t know.

After Ronnie’s experience, I believe that we all have guardian angels but maybe we’re not receptive enough to see or feel them or to know that they have actually intervened on our behalf. We tend to think that all is coincidence.

EPILOGUE: *Although the last time he saw Wendy was in his dream two years ago, he is still able to describe her.*

"She had blond hair, she was wearing white, and she was glowing. She had white wings and a nice face. She made me feel happy."

FATHERS AND SONS

My grandmother was an RN in England and professed to have "second sight". Strange things have happened in my life, making me wonder if I have it too.

My husband and I had been married for almost two years. We were living on the east coast and were very happy in our new home. One afternoon I was working in the garden, enjoying the brilliant autumn sunshine with our six-month-old son, when suddenly I developed a violent headache and an ache in my lower left leg. How strange, I thought. What could this be? I glanced at my watch; it was 4:16 P.M. I had to go in and lay down, my wriggling infant beside me.

Moments later, a policeman knocked on my door. My husband had just been killed in a car accident, he told me. While the officer was sorry for my loss, he said that my husband's body would have to be identified.

Where?

In the city morgue!

In total shock, I couldn't bring myself to go. My father went on my behalf.

Some three weeks later, I contacted the local coroner as I had many unanswered questions swimming around in my mind.

"What exactly did my husband die of?

"He died from massive head injuries. He also had a broken left leg." That was news to me.

"What time did the accident happen?"

"Four sixteen P.M.," he replied.

That was the exact time that I developed my severe headache and the ache in my left leg. This was strange to say the least. It was like the day American President Kennedy was shot -- you remember exactly where you were. This was the same thing.

As the years went by, I eventually remarried, moved out west and had two more sons. But I always had an intense fear for the safety of my first son. At first I thought it was natural to be concerned and perhaps a little over-protective because I had lost his father when he was an infant. I didn't want anything to happen to him and I constantly worried about him, much more so than for my two younger sons. I always had a feeling that I was going to lose him. I didn't know how, why, or when, but I always *knew* that something terrible was going to happen to him.

Whenever I cautioned him to be careful his standard answer was a smiling, "Don't worry, Mom. I can take care of myself. I'm a big boy!"

Nonetheless, I'd repeat my admonitions to be cautious despite his slight annoyance. He was extremely outgoing and full of life, always happy, one of these people who never met a stranger. That's just the way he was, so energetic, always doing something.

As time went on, I realized that it wasn't just my fear that was at work here. It was a *knowing* from deep within myself. *I knew something was going to happen to my oldest son.* I never told anybody because I was afraid they would think something was wrong with me.

And then, three days before Christmas, in 1988, it happened. My son, the one that was an infant when his father died, was killed in a car accident. He was seventeen years, eleven months, and one day. So both he and his father were killed in car accidents.

Strange as it sounds, I was almost relieved because I had worried about him so much during his life, and then after his death, I knew I never had to worry about him anymore. I don't mean to sound callous, because that's not what I intend -- I would have given my life to save him. It's just that I never felt that way about either of my other sons.

There are very few people that I told about my foreboding. Actually my sister is the only one, because I know how cold-hearted it sounds. That's not what I mean, but I'm afraid that's how people will interpret it.

I was holding my breath for seventeen years waiting for something dreadful to happen and then it happened! It's very strange to look back on the feelings I had then, and now to be aware -- and thankful -- that I no longer have them.

Where I got that dreadful knowledge from, I don't know but I thought it must have been from my deceased husband. Did he impart those feelings to me? That's how I looked at it anyhow. After the funeral, I spoke to my deceased husband: "I had our son for almost 18 years. Now it's your turn. Now you've got him."

It's comforting because I know he is with his father now. I've come to terms with it. I don't know why my son died and I don't know why my husband died, but there has to be a reason. They were both very young. They both died in car accidents. They were both travelling in the same direction (south-east). They both died of head injuries. They each had a broken left leg.

There were three vehicles involved in each accident. Two cars and a big dump truck became entangled when my husband died. In my son's case, it was a full-sized van and two cars. There were so many similarities.

Everything in my life seems to happen in three's. When my son was killed, he was skiing with two friends and the three of them were driving from Lake Louise to Banff, where they planned to spend the night. The accident was so bad they couldn't even tell who was driving. All three boys were killed in the 1981 Thunderbird.

There happened to be three doctors driving along close behind them. Each doctor went to one of the boys and I found that really comforting. You always wonder if they would have survived had they gotten to the hospital sooner, but deep inside I know that wouldn't have helped. I think something like this is supernatural; it didn't happen randomly.

I would not wish this experience on my worst enemy. It changed my life and has made me a totally different person. A lot of my problems seem extremely petty now and I've developed an appreciation for many different things. I believe we are the sum of our life's experiences.

Even though I'm not a churchgoer, I have a very deep belief system. A lot of people lose faith when something tragic like that happens, but with me it was the opposite. Because my son was so vital, I believe he couldn't have been wiped out for no reason, even if I don't understand the rationale yet.

There really is more to heaven and earth than meets the eye but many people are afraid. After I lost my husband and my teenage son, I desperately needed to see them again. I wanted to have a visitation or some other confirmation of their continued existence in my life.

I've always encouraged them in my thoughts and talked aloud to both of them, even though it's twenty-five years since my husband died. He's buried on the other side of the country but my son is buried here and I talk to him whenever I visit the cemetery.

I don't handle birthdays particularly well at any time but my fortieth one was extremely difficult. I was having a *really bad day* and would have jumped off a cliff without a second thought, had one been handy. I decided to go to the cemetery and left work early so it wouldn't be too dark when I got there.

At the cemetery I sobbed, my heart breaking, the words to my dead son barely coherent.

"I don't know if I can go on anymore," I sobbed. "Are you listening to me? Can you hear me? Let me know if you can hear me," I pleaded through my tears.

Then out of nowhere, I heard church bells ringing. There is no church with bells even remotely close to that cemetery. In all the years I have been going to the cemetery, I have never before heard them and I knew I was not just hearing things.

I stood there with joy in my heart. The answer to my prayers. Now, I knew I had the strength to go on.

So why do good people die so young and evil people live forever? Why do these things happen? I'm not sure when I heard the answer, but it probably was after my husband died.

The answer can be explained by looking at a piece of needlepoint. First look at the picture on the front, then hold it over your head so it is to the light. When you look at the underside, all the threads are going in different, random directions and you can't make out the image. But God is looking down at the picture side and can see the whole finished picture.

I always think of that now because there must be a definite plan, a complete picture. There's a finished product there and every one of those random threads makes up a part of the overall. We just can't see it yet…

I used to do needlepoint and I recall that on one in particular, there were a lot of black and red threads, and I couldn't make out the sleek, black panther gazing at the beautiful red flowers on the other side. I was only able to see random colours.

We always search for ways to explain events in our lives.

SECOND CHANCE

It wasn't until I was a mother myself and my own prayers were answered in what I can only call a miracle, that I fully understood my mother and her constant sadness as I was growing up. I certainly was more understanding of the tragedy that happened in her life and could see how easily these things can happen.

Mother was a new war bride with two children, one thirteen months old and one nine months older than that. It was Friday and Friday was cleaning day. She had a neighbour who lived next door, a maiden lady who was much older than her and whom she always called Miss Shaunessey.

Mother was wearing the emerald green dress that she loved. The occasion was a visit and a cup of tea with Miss Shaunessey in mid-afternoon. Then because my father was expected home from work at five o'clock and wanting his dinner, Mother rushed around to get the cleaning done.

Rather than put cold water in the pail and then add boiling water from the kettle like she usually did, she poured the scorching water from the kettle into the pail first and then went to the sink to get the cold water. My sister Sarah was tugging on Mother's skirt and as Mother turned from the sink, Sarah fell into the pail of scalding water. She died that night.

My mother never forgave herself for losing her firstborn to that accident. She always said that if she hadn't been talking to Miss Shaunessey, she never would have been rushing around like that, and Sarah wouldn't have died. For the rest of her life, Mother never made up with the neighbour, never had a friend, and she became a very private person. A recluse really.

It coloured her entire life and created a rift between her and my father that never healed. There was a palpable distance between them. And although I'm sure he forgave her, she could never forgive herself. She became an overprotective mother. We were never allowed to do anything -- we could never have a bike, we could never roller-skate, we could never go to Niagara Falls.

All alone in a strange country, Mother carried this burden of guilt for her entire life. Back in England, she was the youngest of fifteen children in a combined family after her mother had married for the second time. My father had grown up in the same village. He came to Canada with his brother when he was just a lad, and later joined the Canadian army and went overseas during WW1.

In the meantime my mother had grown up and they were married in 1918 after the war was over. Because my father had to return to Canada to be discharged, they decided to make their fortune here and then return home to England. Of course they never got back home because they never made a fortune. Mother returned only after Father died many years later.

So when my little sister died, Mother was all alone in a strange country with no family. The only correspondence was by letter and that took about six weeks. It was a different world then and my mother had a very hard life. She never wore green again. She declared that it was an unlucky colour for her.

I have two older brothers. I remember my childhood as being very sad and not really understanding why. Every Sunday was a trip to the cemetery to put flowers on my sister's grave. We watched silently as my mother wept. When the Great Depression came along, I was five years old and my father lost his job. From my earliest memories through to my tenth year was a very sad time.

These things happen to people every day but we never fully understand the consequences. We see something in the paper and think that must be awful for that particular family, but unless you're part of the scene, you can't possibly understand how truly awful it really is.

We had a very solitary upbringing despite the fact that we always lived in town. Social graces are all foreign to me. The things that come easily to people because they were part of their growing-up years, I know nothing about. We had no extended family and there were no neighbours. My mother saw to that. She would never go beyond saying a brisk "Good morning" to a neighbour over the back fence and that was the end of that.

She became very superstitious. If we broke a mirror, it was gloom in our house and she'd wait for something bad to happen so she could blame it on the broken mirror. Obviously something was bound to happen sooner or later.

I guess time helped a bit but the situation never really turned around. Every year, Mother would say, "Sarah would have been ten today" or "Sarah would have been fifteen today." When my mother was dying she said, "Sarah would have been sixty now." She never got over it and all of our lives were affected as a consequence.

Nonetheless, my brothers and I eventually grew up. It was after I was married that I had a strange experience with our own four-year-old son Charlie, one that helped me to understand, at least in part, what my mother had gone through.

My husband and I had had a party. Being new parents and rather unaware, we had left a bowl of salted peanuts on the table. Charlie ran over and crammed his mouth full of peanuts. He choked a bit but then seemed to be okay. We didn't think too much of it at the time.

But what was persistent hacking turned into a dreadfully nasty cough within twenty-four hours, so I called the doctor and told him what had happened. He said, "We'd better get an X-ray of his chest."

The X-ray clearly showed that a peanut was firmly lodged in his lung. The doctor admitted Charlie to the hospital because of fear that peanut oil pneumonia could develop. I guess the peanut was an irritant. He went on to say that if it did develop, Charlie would be in serious trouble because this pneumonia didn't respond to any of the known antibiotics.

The doctors didn't want to do anything about getting the peanut out, they never really did say why. But Charlie went on to develop peanut oil pneumonia and there was no treatment.

He was very frail and not doing well, breathing shallowly, and sweating with a fever that spiked right off the chart. I could see him deteriorating before my eyes. They more or less said that there was very little hope. I thought he was going to die. Things were very dark.

Every day I stayed with him and helplessly watched him slip further and further away from me. How could we have been so stupid as to put those damn peanuts out?

On the fourth day, I went like every other morning, fearful that the worst had happened. When I got there, the nurses were helping a healthy-looking Charlie get dressed to come home.

"What happened?" I asked, too stunned to believe what I was seeing.

The doctor said, "Nobody knows, and please don't ask. We X-rayed him again this morning and there's no peanut there. His temperature's gone down and we can't find anything wrong with him."

I hugged my little boy, tears streaming down my face.

"Why are you crying Mommy?" Charlie asked.

"Mommy's happy that you're better, sweetie-pie," I said.

I couldn't believe it. My prayers had been answered. The doctor said there was no explanation. "Just accept it," he said.

To me, it truly was a miracle. I had no other explanation. I think that everyone has their own religion whether it's formal or not. We all believe in something, the power of something bigger than ourselves.

I felt grateful for a second chance. I swore that nothing like this would ever happen again, especially something that was my own fault. This had been precipitated by carelessness even though it was not intentional. I felt this was a warning.

Like my own mother, I became overprotective of my kids after that. I know all too well how these things can affect you.

CHAPTER SEVEN

ξ NURSES & OTHER HEALERS ξ

...The sharp compassion of the healer's art
Resolving the enigma of the fever chart.
T.S. Eliot (1888 – 1965)

Nurses are among the most admired of all professionals. Nurses are caring, nurses are compassionate. Nurses have a gentle touch quite unlike that of anyone else, including in the middle of the night, 24/7.

The goal of nurses is to help their patients become whole in body, mind, and spirit, often under challenging circumstances, and to seek the most satisfactory outcome possible. If a cure is not to be, the caring remains.

Nurses and other healers have always automatically used their hands in providing care. Who has not been comforted in a scary situation by having someone holding their hand, whether it's a little boy getting stitches for a gash in his forehead or someone older with a fractured hip after a fall on an icy sidewalk.

The intangible tools -- a freshness of spirit, a nice smile, a sense of humour, all are in the therapeutic repertoires of most nurses. Innately, they know their intrinsic value in the healing arts. Sometimes what is needed most is a sympathetic ear and genuine empathy. Caring!

One of the formal tools nurses use is Therapeutic Touch. This scientifically-based process was developed by Dr. Dolores Krieger RN and Dora Kunz in 1972 and starts out with an assessment of an individual's energy field. Another tool is the Healing Touch program which was developed in 1990 and involves a variety of different techniques.

I once worked with an RPN who, before entering the nursing profession, made his living breaking into people's homes and stealing all their good stuff. He said if someone unexpectedly came home before he had a chance to run off with the loot, he'd very consciously suck in his energy and thus remain undetected. When the coast was clear, he'd take off. He actually was a very good RPN.

Writer Janet Fitch says that if she were a poet, she would write about, "People who worked in the middle of the night... emergency room nurses with their gentle hands... they knew how long the night was... Night workers lived without illusions, they wiped dreams off counters..."[xv]

There are also other healers, some of whom are mystical and tender and kind, and work in mysterious ways with various energies.

THIRD ROOM FROM THE END

Had I not been personally involved, I would have just blown it off as a story that was making the rounds. I was working as a Registered Nurse for the summer in a very old hospital that had previously been used for Second World War veterans.

The main "L" shape of the hospital that previously was used as patient care wards had been renovated into testing labs and endoscopy suites. The branches that went off the long part of the "L" remained the current patient care areas.

There were five wings: A, B, C, D, and E, and I was working on the D wing. When I looked out the windows on one side, I could see the E wing and from the windows on the other side I could see the C wing. They were all identically built so that if I was doing a dressing for instance, I had to pull the drapes on the windows because you could see right through to the next wing, even though it was maybe seventy-five yards away.

When they began the renovations in 1982, they started in A wing, totally encased it in tarps and plastic, gutted the interior, and left only the exterior structure. When each wing was completed, the results were absolutely gorgeous. When I was there, only A and B were finished.

For years, C wing had been used for chronic care and psychiatry. Now it was totally encased but no active construction was being done because the money had run out, and so it stayed.

REGISTERED NURSE

It was on my eighth night in a row that I heard the same story that every other night nurse had heard. Years ago, a nurse had been doing her night rounds on C wing. She got as far as the third window from the end when she was murdered. A psychiatric patient had jumped her and slit her throat! This was shortly after the Second World War.

Oh really. Nice little tale.

One night on D2, which was the second floor of the D wing, I was checking on one of my ophthalmology patients. I looked out the window and saw a light going from room to room on the second floor of the closed C wing. The light continued until it got to the third window from the end, where it was mysteriously extinguished. I whipped out of the room and breathlessly called to my nursing colleague, "There's a light on in C2! Come and see."

Of course by then everything was pitch black.

Calmly she told me that the light appears on the 19th day of every month at three o'clock in the morning, the exact date and time that the nurse was murdered.

"It might have been a security guard doing his checks," I said hopefully.

"No," she explained. "Nobody can get into C wing. Don't worry, she's just making her rounds. It's always the same pattern."

When I stopped shaking, I realized that the light wasn't like the concentrated beam from our halogen flashlights. Rather, it was more like the glow you get from a candle, with a softer, wider and more diffuse beam.

Nonetheless when the supervisor came around, I asked her about the light. "Do you think it was Security?"

"No, there's nobody in there. C wing is totally sealed off. This is something that just happens. Wish her well."

She went on to tell me that the story of the psychiatric patient killing the night nurse in the third room from the end was definitely true.

I thought they had been pulling my leg -- until I saw the light.

THIS OLD HOUSE

For five years after the death of my first husband, I continued to work as a Registered Nurse. When I remarried, my new husband and I decided to buy a new home together. We found one we both liked that was about twenty years old. It was built back in the '50's.

At first everything seemed okay, but as my husband's work took him out of town more and more, I noticed that strange things started happening when he was gone. For instance, the downstairs light would turn on and off by itself.

The bedroom light was something else. I would wake up in the middle of the night and the bedroom light would be on. It wasn't just that the bulb was glowing -- the wall switch would be flipped into the ON position. If I went to bed and purposely left the light on, I'd wake up and it would be off and the switch would also be in the OFF position. I told my husband about the lights and he said, "It's just a short." I knew it wasn't a short because the switch kept changing position too.

The doorbell would ring, half-ring, that is. It was one of those two-tone doorbells that ring once when you push it in and then ring again on a lower tone when you take your finger off. Rather like the DING-DONG of the Avon lady. But it would only DING! I tried to make it ring once like that, but it wouldn't work. I got the normal DING-DONG every time. And it only happened when my husband was out of town. I wasn't scared or nervous. I just thought it all very bizarre.

My young son always slept with his brown teddy bear and in our first night in that house, he slept comfortably with his favourite toy tucked under his arm. But the next night we couldn't find it anywhere. The teddy bear had mysteriously disappeared. I called my mother to talk to her about it since we all knew that my son had his teddy bear that first night. She had no answers for us.

Six months later, my husband was being transferred out west and we were getting ready to move again. It was then that we found the teddy bear in a box that had never been unpacked.

The same thing happened with a pair of scissors that I used for the first couple of days before they went missing. Again I found them six months later, in a box that had never been opened, albeit a different box than the one we found the missing teddy bear in. That made me a little nervous after the fact. I thought, the scissors go missing and I find them here?

I got pregnant while we were in that house and along with the lights going on and off and the doorbell DINGING instead of DING-DONGING, there were two instances that stand out in my mind. If I close my eyes I can see them happening all over again because they were so weird.

Still working as an RN, I decided to have a short nap before going in for another busy 3-11 shift. While I was lying down, the telephone beside my bed rang once. I put my hand out to pick it up but the receiver leapt out of the cradle and lay on the table beside the phone, right in front of me. It startled me so much I started to laugh.

I picked up the phone and it was my sister-in-law, my first husband's sister on the phone. "Look," I said in the midst of my nervous laughter, "I can't talk to you right now. I'll phone you right back," and with that I hung up. It was at least ten minutes before I was able to stop laughing and call her back. Thankfully, that only happened to me the one time.

The second incident happened when I was sitting at the kitchen table and decided to clean out my purse -- you know how we collect all this stuff.

I picked up all the junk and had both hands full of Kleenex, bits of tape, and other assorted things. I turned around, looked at the cupboard underneath the kitchen sink where my garbage container was and thought, *oh great, why didn't I open the cupboard before I picked this stuff up. My hands are full and how am I going to get the cupboard door open now?*

Well -- the cupboard door just opened by itself. Stunned, I looked up and said "thank you." I didn't know what else to do. I never told my husband about the flying phone or the opening cupboard door.

Despite these inexplicable happenings, I didn't have any uncomfortable feelings, chills, or sensation of any ghostly presences. Somehow I just thought it was the house. The house I had lived in previously was one I had really loved, but the bizarre thing was that my sister always said that this house, even with all the weird things going on, was the most comfortable house she had ever been in and she absolutely loved to spend time in it. Why, she couldn't say.

I think people thought that I was very peculiar but I'm the one who lived there. I know these things happened. So when people have odd experiences, I listen with an open mind because I've had unusual experiences of my own.

I wasn't in the house long enough to do any historical research although I would have liked to. However, shortly after we moved in, one of the neighbours said, "How do you like the new house?"

Before I could answer, he said something I was to think of later, "You know, strange things happen in there."

I don't know if he was referring to the family that had lived there before or to the house itself.

The way I sold the house wasn't supernatural, but it certainly was curious. After moving out west, we rented it out for a time prior to deciding to sell it. Before I had time to contact anyone, I got a phone call from the real estate agent that we had bought the house through originally. He said that the son of the woman we bought the house from now wanted to buy it back. And that's how the house was sold. Talk about perfect timing.

Or was it something else?

PETER ©

Peter was a dear friend of mine, from many years ago. We were best mates all through high school. I had not seen him for fifteen years, when I bumped into him by accident in a tavern, near where I used to work, several years ago. I was on afternoon shift and used to call in there occasionally, on a hot night, for a quick beer on my way home. We recognized each other and sat together at the bar, getting reacquainted, until closing time.

Peter was married with four children and had a very good job as a toolmaker. But it shortly became obvious to me that Peter was an alcoholic. He'd been living at the tavern for the past couple of weeks since his wife had thrown him out. Peter was a quiet, gentle, happy drunk, and was never violent or aggressive. He loved his wife and children dearly, and desperately wanted to go home, but for the life of him he could not stop drinking.

Heading off to his room we sat and talked much of the night away. I explained a little to Peter about my life, and the mystical, research and healing work I was doing. I offered to give him healing, hoping I could help him in some way and, with an amused smile and a twinkle in his eye, he accepted my offer. While we were talking in the half dark of his small room, I observed his aura.

There was almost nothing left of Peter's main aura. His etheric was not detectable at all and there was only the merest hint of pale-blue, with a few silver sparkles floating about in the faint auric cloud around him. This was not detectable with normal auric sight, and I had to really strain to see it. I was amazed at what I could see. I had seen the auras of many people, and plenty of alcoholics, but had never seen anything quite like this one before. I asked after his health, which he said was excellent -- apart from the occasional hangover. Peter was a keen sportsman, but also a binge drinker. He would often go for weeks, drinking only a few cans of beer a day, and then he'd binge for a few days and totally wipe himself out. I was amazed he'd managed to hold down a steady job, but Peter said he never actually drank at work, even when he was bingeing. He often went to work drunk, but his mates always covered up for him, and his luck had held out so far… he said laughing.

My intuition prompted me that something important was happening and I suspected, sadly, that Peter did not have long to live. This, I felt, was why we had bumped into each other again, after so many years. There are, my life's experience has taught me, no real coincidences in this world.

I told him all of this and it did not faze him in the slightest. He agreed with me, feeling something strange was happening within himself, but he did not really care - he was so very unhappy. We talked late into the night about his problems. He had, basically, never got over the death of his mother, which happened when he was a young boy, a few years before we'd met. He blamed her death on himself, for some obscure reason, and that was why he drank so much. He knew this was stupid and illogical but he couldn't help the way he felt. He felt terribly guilty inside and did not think he deserved to be happy or even to live a normal life. He wasn't consciously trying to ruin his life by being an alcoholic, but the depression and urge to drink, when it came, was so very strong he just couldn't fight it anymore. The booze stopped his depression, while he stayed drunk, but the effect on his outside life and family was devastating.

We sat facing each other and I meditated for a short time then gave Peter deep healing. The amount of energy that flooded through me made me gasp, and the room swam around me. I almost passed out, it was that intense. Peter was totally stunned by the energy he felt coming through me into him. As this happened, the room around us faded half from sight and the air filled with soft, textured white cloud, with shafts of flickering silvery light coming from our left. Suddenly, standing beside us, were Peter's mother and father.

Peter had never seen anything like this before, and was totally amazed and profoundly moved by it all. His mother touched his face and he reached out and touched hers. They gazed into each other's eyes for some time. Peter's father stood there beside them, smiling down at him. Peter looked at me with astonishment, then back at his mother and father, and then promptly burst into tears, sobbed uncontrollably. His mother looked up at me for a moment, giving me such a sweet, sad little smile, moving me deeply.

The clouds faded away and the room returned to normal a few seconds later. Peter was so moved and uplifted by this experience he was galvanized with energy and purpose. He swore to me he would never drink again, and would go and seek medical help if the depression came back - and I totally believed him. His aura was much brighter and full of energy, but was unchanged from its pale blue colour and lack of etheric border. Peter, now stone cold sober, showered and dressed while I made more coffee. He came out clean-shaven, wearing nice clothes and looking years younger. We finished our coffee and said our good-byes, then he hurried home to his wife and children. It was getting close to dawn by now, and looked like it was going to be a great day.

His wife took him back immediately, probably awed at the great change in him. He phoned me a few days later, to thank me and let me know he was OK - knowing I was worried about him. I could hear his wife and children laughing and giggling in the background. I asked him how he felt, and he said he'd never felt better or happier in his entire life. Peter wanted to get together and discuss what had happened between us on that special night. He had not told anyone about what had happened. He was a Catholic and did not know how to even begin explaining it to his family. We made arrangements to meet a few days later.

Two days later, Peter awoke in the early hours of the morning, complaining of a terrible headache. A blood vessel in his brain had burst. He died in his wife's arms on the way to hospital.

Robert Bruce, mystic & author, Australia

THE FOREVER CHEST ©

Jenny was a lovely, gentle lady I once knew. She was a young mother, with three happy children and a loving husband. One day Jenny slipped in the shower and fell onto the raised brick side of the basin. She had massive bruising right next to her anus.

Several months later she developed cancer of the bowel, and the first tumour appeared, partially protruding, right next to where the bruising from her fall had been. She fought this terrible disease for five long years with many operations and chemical and radiation treatments, but at the end of this time she had had enough. Jenny had suffered so terribly that she just wanted to die - but was so very terrified of death.

I was introduced to Jenny, a few short weeks before her death by a healer friend of mine who had been seeing her for some months. I saw Jenny several times before her eventual death. When I first saw her, my heart went out to her - she was incredibly brave - but so very scared of death. One look at her aura and I knew her time was very close and… inevitable.

Her aura was very large, almost four times normal size and the palest of blues, and was virtually undetectable as an aura. It was full of sparkling silver and white sparks that had an effervescent look and feel to it.

All her hair had fallen out and she was bloated and sick from chemotherapy and the merciful, pain-killing drugs she was taking. But within her ravaged body was a tender, loving, and bright spirit looking out at me. When I first looked into Jenny's eyes, her spirit reached out and touched my soul, pleading for help to end her fear and suffering.

This communication was beyond the threshold of normal understanding. Her spirit spoke directly to mine and I realized I knew her well. I had been led back to Jenny to help her. This is hard to understand, I know, but I instantly loved Jenny, as a father loves his daughter. When I left her after the first visit, I drove my battered old

VW Kombi van down a dirt road and parked amongst a grove of Gum trees atop a hill.

This was a special high place for me. I came here whenever I was troubled and wanted to think profoundly. It overlooked the ocean in the distance, a few miles away. I could see the white caps of the waves, catching the sun's rays in the distance, sparkling like pearls amidst a blue gleaming ocean.

I sat there for hours, all the late afternoon, thinking and meditating on Jenny's dilemma and what I could do to help, and the why of it all. I opened myself up to what had just happened and looked at it with deeper eyes. I desperately needed to know how I could heal Jenny's inner pain - that was now my pain. The deep healing I had given her had uplifted and stopped her physical pain. But, oh my God, the pain within that gentle lady. It ate away at her heart and my soul felt bruised and heavy with the sharing of it.

At sunset, while I watched in lonely awe, a spectacular peach sunset filled the skyline, blasting away the last of the day in preparation for the cool of the coming night. At the height of this splendour I got out of my car and knelt in the long grass, facing the setting sun. Here I silently worshipped the great presence that creates all things, which I can sense most strongly in the sun.

I closed my eyes and surrendered myself totally to it and reached out towards it for help. I ceased all my efforts to understand Jenny's dilemma and total acceptance soon filled and opened me.

When the answer came, my eyes gushed tears of thankfulness and relief -- as that great presence found me again -- and silenced the world around me. I felt a heavy, thick, loving hush descend around me. All the birds and insects singing and chirping around me stopped their clamour and looked on in silence, sensing His presence as I was. In utter silence, and in His presence - I suddenly knew what I had to do. This was just like remembering something forgotten. It just popped into my head like it had been there all along.

I had not been led back to Jenny to heal her and make her well. I had been led back to Jenny to give her back her joy and trust and to help her die in peace.

I spent many hours with Jenny over the next few weeks, talking and explaining and healing. Her pain stopped completely after the first healing session, and she was able to stop taking the morphine, which was repressing and clouding her mind. She was amazed and uplifted and actually forgot, on many occasions, that she was so very sick and swiftly dying. She used to laugh and joke about the "phantom illness" that was "sort of" killing her.

In this short time, I worked steadily at preparing Jenny for death. Normally, as a healer, I am always hopeful and try to pass on a feeling of confidence to the patient. I try and get them to face one day at a time and rarely mention death - but don't avoid the subject. I was honest with Jenny, and told her she was dying, and began teaching

Jenny everything I knew about life and death - and a lot more I didn't know I knew which was given to me as I spoke.

I told her all my old stories and jokes and experiences. I told these so well and so vividly that Jenny lived them with me, sharing them on a soul deep level - and we began to remember more about each other, from other times we had met. Jenny drank deeply of my life and her soul thrived on my memories and mystical experiences and joy and her spirit grew steadily stronger.

I explained the death process to Jenny in minute detail and what would happen to her during and after her passing. She listened carefully and was very brave. During this time I also used my mystical powers to great effect, and implanted seeds within her subconscious mind that would soon burst forth into her conscious mind in the coming days. These were designed to hammer home the truth and reality of the wonderful experience she was about to have.

Jenny's death was very special. I do not know why, and cannot even begin to explain it - it is far beyond my humble understanding of reality. All I know is that this death was very special and important to Jenny's soul.

We laughed a lot and cried a lot together as well, during the few, precious hours we spent together - mostly tears of joy shared. But, my work was soon done, and done well. When I last saw Jenny, the day before her collapse, she was radiant and full of joy. All I had been telling her had surfaced within and had been made real to her being. Her faith became a shining, effervescent fountain.

Jenny was so close to spirit that she was seeing some of the wonderful things I had been preparing her for. Her much loved grandmother was with her constantly. They talked a lot -- when no one could hear them. Her grandmother had been dead for over ten years, but she had come back to help with Jenny's passing. Jenny had missed her so and was absolutely thrilled to see her again.

The last thing Jenny said to me was that if she could be with her beloved grandmother, whom she adored, dying was well worth it. And that if she had the power to change anything about her life and the present - she would not do so now. She totally accepted her life and coming death. She seemed to understand it, although she could not put it into words - it just felt right to her.

Jenny was laughing quietly under her hand and had a knowing twinkle in her eyes that only I understood, when we said our last good-bye. We had a huge good-bye cuddle that day. She was so happy and looking forward to her coming experience. She knew she was going to die very, very soon, but was not scared anymore. She knew her family would survive without her and would, one day, dry their tears and get on with their lives again. She was content and ready to surrender her body when the time came. Jenny had got her smile back.

Jenny collapsed with respiratory failure and was rushed to

hospital later that day. She never recovered consciousness again and passed peacefully away four days later. I did not go to her funeral.

But wait, the story does not end here, nor so sadly…

Two weeks later I was meditating, as was my practice then, in the late evening. I had just reached the trance state and starting some energy work, when a feeling came over me, a premonition that something major was about to happen. Shortly after this, there came an enormous flood of pure, source energy into the room. This is unmistakable for what it is, pure silver energy from a very high level - the spirit world.

I looked up, opening my other eyes, and there appeared a large rent in the dimensional veil - of the nicer kind - opposite me. Jenny stepped through the rift and, hanging on to her grandmother for dear life, was waving and yelling and laughing and jumping up and down and blowing me kisses and hugs. She looked so radiant and happy and was very beautiful. All her lovely, long black hair was back and she was at her most magnificent and radiant.

The joy coming through the ether, directed at me, was incredibly powerful and oh, so very moving. I waved back and blew her kisses, wiping away my tears with my other hand. Then Jenny stopped, moved closer to me, and smiled such a beautiful smile at me. I saw, in Jenny's eyes, the same happy, knowing look I had seen in them the last time I had seen her. She blew me one last kiss and with a final wave the veil closed around her and the room returned to normal.

Who said being a poor, starving mystic has no rewards in this world. For that sweet, loving smile, my friends, was a priceless jewel, a reward far beyond any price. I would not trade that one, sweet smile, for anything -never! I will take my treasures with me when I leave this world. They will always be with me, tucked away in my heart… forever. I have a special little treasure chest, deep within my heart, where I store these precious, timeless little jewels. I call it my "forever chest."

Robert Bruce, mystic & author, Australia

INVISIBLE VISITORS

As a Registered Nurse working in the Intensive Care Unit, many of my patients were seriously ill. Occasionally I had a patient who was dying and I knew that there was nothing more to be done for him, like resuscitation or any of those other so-called heroics. At that time, nobody got into a panic about pumping a patient's chest until forever and putting him on a respirator.

The dying patient would be lying there alone in his room, unconscious, but I could sense that he was not really alone. I could not see the visitors but I could *feel* them. If this sensation at the bedside was very strong, I knew that there was more than one invisible visitor.

One night I had a female patient who was dying and the staff nurse I was working with said, "She's so agitated. Something's wrong over there. Shall I go and stay with her?"

"No," I said. "She's got some company. I think we better leave her be."

The nurse looked at me with big eyes. She had heard that I had extra "sensitivities," but this was the first time she had worked with me. A little while later, my patient died peacefully.

As in many hospitals, the Recovery Room was next door to the Intensive Care Unit. At night after all the surgery had been completed for the day, the Recovery Room of course would be empty. The only reason we would go there in the off hours would be to pick up some needed equipment.

One evening, two staff nurses came tearing out of the Recovery Room, looking scared out of their wits. I could sense that someone was trotting right behind them as they ran back into ICU.

Now I couldn't see whoever it was behind them but I could *feel* it because my skin started to grow, I got goose bumps, and my hair was rising up on my head.

"Come and sit down," I said to the nurses. "Have a cup of tea."

To the invisible visitors I said, "Perhaps you'd better go back to rest."

"What on earth is happening here?' asked the petrified nurses.

"Aahhh, nothing. Nothing's happening."

Strange but true. Most of my experiences in that line have been very good. I feel my hair rise and I know somebody's there but it doesn't scare me.

Only twice or thrice in my life have I had an experience in the hospital that I would call evil. When that happens, *I know!* I feel very afraid deep inside, as if there's *something* there that shouldn't be there. In those instances, what I do is bless myself and say a prayer. The bad feeling always goes away.

At home, I've never had an experience that I could call evil, but if I dream of snakes it means that someone is going to do something that will affect me in a negative way. If a snake actually bites me, something extremely bad always happens to me within a couple of weeks.

I don't know why this is.

HOLY HORNETS

We had gone to Midland and then on to the Stations of the Cross. Neither my husband nor I are Catholic but this was something we wanted to do. Tommy, my ten-year-old stepson, was with us. We bought some Holy Water that I put in my purse, and continued walking towards the restaurant. My husband went into the restaurant to get a carryout lunch while Tommy and I sat down at a table, waiting for him.

Suddenly Tommy started screaming at the top of his lungs. I couldn't understand what was wrong with him. He pointed to his arm in horror and there was a huge hornet!

I pulled off his T-shirt to find his arms and chest completely covered by hornets and extremely nasty-looking welts. Tommy was shrieking so loudly that I didn't know what to do. Then, thinking that kids are kids, I said, "Hang on a second, Tommy. I'll put some Holy Water on these bites and you won't have any more problems."

I took the Holy Water out and sprinkled it all over him. By the time his father got back, there wasn't a mark on him. We couldn't believe it.

I've had other things happen where I have a sense of *knowing*. I have a business phone at home and occasionally when I go out I'll say to my husband, "Don't worry about the phone. It won't ring until I'm back and you hear me putting my key in the door."

And that's what happens. Something just comes over me and I know.

I'm in the nursing agency business and sometimes it's slow and we don't have a lot of business. Then I might get a flash of insight and say, "We're going to get a phone call in about ten minutes and it's going to be a new private duty case for us."

And that's exactly what happens.

UNPAID HELP

In the style of the time, the medical/palliative care ward at the general hospital where I used to work as an RN had lots of nooks and crannies. The ghost stories from the past lingered and when we had patients who were old enough to remember when this floor used to be the psychiatric ward, they'd really get freaked out. The doors were solid oak with portals and skeleton keys were required to lock them.

We usually had forty very heavy patients and they each required an extreme amount of care. There were patients requiring palliative care, isolation (before universal precautions) and there were many terminally ill patients with various medical problems such as Lou Gehrig's Disease (ALS) and multiple sclerosis (MS).

On the night shift, we made our routine rounds at 1 A.M., at 3 A.M., and at 5 A.M. and usually a round would take between one-and-a-half to two hours, so we were essentially doing rounds all night. There were three of us on, plus sometimes we would get an orderly to help.

One night we were doing our 3A.M. rounds in the far reaches of the ward when one of the call bells came on from the other corridor. We were headed in that direction anyway, so we decided to ignore the bell for a few minutes until we got there.

We knew the two ladies in that room were basically in a vegetative state. One couldn't speak at all and the other, larger patient muddled in and out of a state of confusion. Neither of them could get themselves to the bathroom, nor could they get onto a bedpan by themselves. In fact, they each required a minimum of two nurses to get them onto a bedpan.

It took us a bit longer than we thought so I sent one of the RNA's to investigate. She came back white as a sheet. She said that the larger of the two patients was already on the bedpan.

Not really expecting an intelligible answer, she nonetheless asked the patient who put her on the pan. In a rare moment of lucidity, the patient described a short grey-haired nurse who was wearing an old style nurses' cap, one in the form of a cupcake. Her grey hair was neatly pulled back in a bun. She wore a starched apron over a white uniform and carried a big bunch of skeleton keys.

We knew nobody else was on the ward because there were buzzers on every door to guard against patients who were "wanderers." No buzzers had gone off and we knew there were only the four of us there. Certainly none of the other patients could have put this patient on the bedpan.

When I spoke to the patient myself, she kept repeating, "Such a nice nurse!" over and over again, smiling. I had chills down my spine but I went out to the corridor and called out, "Anytime you want to come back and help, please do. We can use all the help we can get."

In the morning, we told our head nurse of the night's events. Very superstitious, she was from the old school and didn't doubt our story at all. She was adamant that our ghost was one of the nurses who had previously worked there and had either returned or else had never left.

The next few nights, I found myself discreetly watching over my shoulder. There unquestionably had been many strange stories up to that point. Some of the nurses swore they heard jingling keys in the corridor when no one was there, while others claimed to have caught a glimpse of someone. It was very common for nurses to feel someone behind them as they walked down the long corridors to answer a call bell.

How do I explain it? It's just one of those quirky things.

CALL WAITING

The ward where I worked as a Registered Nurse was broken up into two wings. The one wing was square with the rooms running around the outside and on the inside were a shower and tubs, a walkway and a treatment room. The other wing was a just long hall that ran straight down. If we were on one side, we couldn't see the other. I don't know why anyone would ever design it this way.

The nurses' station was right smack dab in the centre of this. When we sat at the nurses' station, we could not see any of the patients' rooms. If we went out of the nurses' station and turned to the back hallway and turned left once more, there was a shower stall that backed right onto the nurses' station. The shower no longer worked and the call bell had been disconnected long ago. We used the area to stock adult diapers and other supplies.

Before I started working there, a patient who was in the shower had had a heart attack and pulled the call bell. Because of the way the ward was designed, the staff didn't find the patient until it was too late. He had died, call bell in hand. The time was 2 P.M.

Now here's the wild thing about it. Ever since that happened, that call bell would periodically go off at 2 P.M. some afternoons. It used to give us the creeps because we couldn't get the bell to turn off. And there was no way to turn it off anyhow, because it had already been disconnected. We called the maintenance department but after checking the wiring, they could find no feasible explanation.

Because our ward provided palliative care, there were a lot of deaths occurring on a fairly routine basis. We soon got to know the meaning of that disconnected call bell ringing at double speed (urgent) when it came on at any time other than 2 P.M. Within minutes, somebody else on the ward would die. We started to track the times and it was getting pretty scary.

We had a lady who had recently been diagnosed with terminal cancer and she wasn't doing very well. She was already bedridden and could hardly turn over without assistance. In the middle of the night shift, I checked on her and, satisfied I could do nothing else for her, joined my colleagues at the nurses' station for a break at 3 A.M.

All of a sudden, the urgent call bell in her bathroom came on, so we all went running down to see what was going on, thinking maybe she had tried to drag herself to the bathroom.

We turned the bell off and saw that she was still in her bed. But when we checked her, she had just passed away. This place was full of things like that.

We had a patient who had ALS (Lou Gehrig's Disease). She and her husband had been married fifty years and a few days after we told her husband that she was terminal, he was coming up less and less because he was so distraught.

One night on rounds, we discovered that this lady had just passed away and we were waiting for the doctor to come up to pronounce her dead. The phone rang and it was switchboard transferring a call from outside to us. It was this lady's husband.

"She's passed away, hasn't she?" he said. We had not called him yet.

I said, "Yes sir, I'm very sorry to inform you that she has."

"Oh," he said, "that's okay. Not five minutes ago my phone rang at home and she said 'Good-bye, honey.'"

I was stunned. This lady was terminal and there was no way she could have used the phone. She couldn't even speak at this point and she was in a private room. Because we dealt with such events so constantly, especially on night shift, we just said, *yeah, yeah,* or ignored them -- or whatever.

Eventually, they decided to close our ward because of cutbacks. Room 302, the farthest one from the nursing station, was to be renovated and then closed until its new role was reassigned. This room, like all the others on the ward, had a functioning call bell. All except the one in the shower stall, of course.

When the painters and other workers were renovating Room 302, the call bell would come on. It kept ringing to the point that it was distracting and annoying, so they disconnected it.

Then the call bell in the next room started ringing so they disconnected it. They ended up disconnecting all of the call bells because they kept ringing when the workers were there. All the furniture and the phones had already been encased in plastic in readiness for the renovators.

After all the call bells had been disconnected, the phone at the nurses' station started ringing. When they traced the call, it was coming from Room 302. So they disconnected the phone in the room but it still kept ringing at the nurses' station. When it was picked up, there was nothing on the other end but an open line and dead silence.

They disconnected the phone at the nurses' station but at 2 A.M. or 3A.M., switchboard would get a call from the phone in Room 302. Again it would be an open line, but they couldn't disconnect it. The phone itself remained undisturbed, encased as it was in plastic. There was dust and dirt and paint on it. There was no way that someone could have snuck in there and used it. Besides, it had been disconnected.

One night I was working in ICU and had to stop in to switchboard to pick up the key to the morgue at about 2:30 A.M. As I was signing the logbook for the key, it happened. A call from Room 302, the empty room.

The switchboard operator said, "Oh no. Not again."

Just then the night supervisor came along and said, "Can't you disconnect it?" She herself was trained to disconnect it but nothing worked. Finally she told the switchboard operator to get on the line.

"Tell them that we know they're there and that we're not going to leave them behind. They'll be taken care of."

The switchboard operator mumbled "Yeah right," under her breath but she got on the line and did as she was asked. The line clicked dead in a heartbeat and there were no more such calls.

I wouldn't have believed it if I hadn't been there and seen it with my own two eyes.

PERMISSION GRANTED

Non-nurses are always amazed at experiences such as this one, but I've become very accustomed to them.

I was nursing in a hospital in northern Michigan where I had a patient with a fulminating tumour. She was unconscious and the entire family was sitting at her bedside, distraught, tears in their eyes.

"Have you all said your good-byes?" I asked. They silently nodded their assent.

I took my patient's hand and said, "It's okay to go." I named every one in the room and said, "Everyone's here and it's okay to go. Go peacefully."

And she did.

The family went "uuuhhhh," not believing what they had just witnessed.

Usually everyone hears about all the technical details of professional care and nothing about our nursing interventions. Our interactions with patients are extremely important and should never be underestimated.

When my grandfather had a severe stroke, I stayed with him. As I saw him deteriorate into unconsciousness, I lovingly squeezed his hand and said "Grampa, when you're ready to go, it's okay."

He died peacefully a short time later.

This is something that we who work with terminally ill people see all the time. The person who is unconscious almost feels as if he has to entertain his guests or wait for everybody to say their good-byes. Ten minutes after the visitors walk out of the room, he's gone.

Something else that often happens but is not totally explainable is one last chance for dying patients to say their piece. The first time I saw it was with a patient who was totally comatosed for a week. His family had travelled a great distance to see him and were in the room when he suddenly sat up and talked to them coherently and lucidly.

When I entered his room, he said, "How the hell are you?" He startled me so much that I just about had a coronary right then and there myself. A short time ago, this man didn't even respond to painful stimuli. He was like that for two hours when he lapsed back into unconsciousness and died.

It happens so often that we as nurses see it all the time. But other people seldom understand the strength of emotional connections to the family.

"I KNOW YOU!"

I worked in ICU as a Registered Nurse and when it was quiet there, I went to the Emergency Department to help out down there. One night we had a code running in the resuscitation room. A male patient had come in VSA, i.e. vital signs absent. He was clinically dead. We did CPR on him, got him back after zapping him a couple of times with the defibrillator and pushing resuscitation drugs intravenously. We shipped him off to the Coronary Care Unit.

After that, I had a couple of days off as did the other nurse who worked with me that night. The E.R. physician went on her vacation. When I returned to work, I went to E.R. again. There was a lab requisition that had to go to CCU so I offered to take it up. This was at the beginning of the evening shift, so I ran up the stairs, still having lots of energy.

As I walked into the CCU, one of the patients called out to me by name. In E.R. we were in the habit of not wearing our names tags or else putting them on backwards because a lot of nurses got harassing phone calls.

This patient was sitting up in bed and I didn't recognize him. "Come here for a minute," he said.

"Hello. Do I know you?"

"I know you! You're the guy who did CPR on me."

At first I thought the other nurses were shining me on, telling stories. Then I realized he was the patient who had coded in E.R. the other night.

"Oh yeah?" I said. "Who told you that?"

"Nobody. I watched you."

"What do you mean you watched me?"

He then proceeded to describe to me in great detail the whole arrest procedure and everything that had happened to him. There were four resuscitation bays, and he knew which one he had been in. He recounted the uniforms we had on, what colour everyone's hair was, and what was said. He had never set foot in our hospital before and even if he had, he would never have been allowed near the resuscitation areas.

I know that hearing is the last sense to go, but this was the first time anyone had ever described a near death experience to me in perfect audio-visual detail. During the next few codes I was involved in, I kept looking up at the ceiling, wondering if we were being watched.

In ICU, the RNA's always made fun of me because whenever I was wrapping bodies up to prepare them for the morgue, I would address them. If I was turning one over to put the shroud under him, I would say, "I'm going to turn you now, Mr. Smith."

I've always had a strong sense within me to do that and I always felt bad when I had to wrap their head in plastic because it somehow didn't seem right to do that so soon after death had occurred.

"This is part of it, Mr. Smith," I'd explain. "It's okay. We'll take care of you."

The RNA's thought I was weird talking to dead people, but it was a sign of respect on my part.

Certainly I've always talked to our gorked patients in ICU. I'd say, "I'm going to turn you over onto your left side now" or I'd tell them what the weather was like outside while I was bathing them. We used to find radios to put in their rooms to keep their minds occupied. I've talked to comatose people and after they regained consciousness, they told me they heard and remembered conversations, so we as nurses have to be careful of what we say.

I like to watch the cardiac monitors when a loved one enters the room. A comatose husband may be really fitful and restless but when the wife comes in and holds his hand, his blood pressure and pulse rate return to normal.

Double blind studies have been done now and the articles indicate that what is said over a patient during anaesthetic influences the outcome. If physicians and nurses say the patient is not going to make it, the patient will have a poorer recovery than if they say the patient is going to do fine. This is regardless of what else is happening. Anaesthetists are encouraged to talk to the patients while they are asleep and surgeons and nurses are discouraged from making jokes about the patient. Soft music is playing during surgery in many operating rooms now as an aid to relaxation and recovery. All this while the patient sleeps…

HAUNTED HOSPITAL

I introduced myself to Hattie in her comfortable apartment, we shook hands, and she asked me to sit down.

"Tell me about yourself," she said.

After detailing a bit about my writing and nursing careers, I could see we weren't through yet. She stretched out her hands, palms upward, and said, "Put your hands on top of mine."

I did. She didn't look at me, and what she focussed on with such intensity, I could not say.

Abruptly she pulled her hands away and smiled.

"Okay," she said.

"Okay what?"

"Just checking your vibes," she said. And so this ICU nurse from British Guyana began to recount her supernatural experiences.

I used to nurse in a very old hospital in Georgetown, British Guyana that was said to be haunted. Various people claimed to have seen a lady who ran around with her robes flying. I've never seen her in my entire life but other things did happen.

I was the primary nurse to a handsome but frail young boy of fourteen who eventually succumbed to leukemia. I felt his loss deeply.

Several nights later, it must have been 5 A.M. when I saw someone bounding up the steps to the second floor, obviously a young boy with lots of energy. He didn't say anything to me or even look in my direction. I thought it a bit odd, but decided it was the paperboy coming extra early. I carried on with my duties.

Shortly after, I took some requisitions to the second floor and asked the nurse there, "Why did the paperboy come so early today?"

"The paperboy?" she said. "He hasn't come yet. We haven't seen anybody."

"He just ran up the steps a few minutes ago," I said. "I saw him."

The minute the words came out of my mouth, I grasped the fact that I'd just seen my young patient who had died from leukemia.

He looked like a real person, not some floating entity. I could *feel* it *now* even though when I saw him, I didn't feel anything at all. When the realization came to me that nobody had come in, I felt creepy, like somebody was touching my skin.

Another time, I took a break during my night shift and wandered down to the front door of the hospital. Even at 3 A.M it was pleasant to look out onto the grounds for a quick breather.

There was a little porch attached to the ward and patients were encouraged to could go out and sit there anytime during the day or evening. Now in the darkness, I could see somebody sitting there, rocking away. It looked like the figure of a man but I didn't recognize him as one of my patients. His face was indistinct in the shadows. I thought, oh heavens, he shouldn't be out of bed at this hour.

I don't like approaching someone when I don't know their name and saying "Hey you! What are you doing there?"

So I walked back to the ward to see who was missing so I could say "Mr. Brown," or "Mr. Whoever, you should be in bed not sitting out there."

We had a long ward with twenty beds on one side and twenty beds on the other. I checked each room. Every patient was accounted for.

Where had this man come from? My heart began beating wildly, out of control: *thump/thump, thump/thump, thump/thump!*

Cautiously I stepped onto the porch. The rocking chair was empty but it still swayed slowly.

"Lord help me," I muttered.

There were more mysterious circumstances in that hospital. One evening as I walked down the corridor, I heard someone call out to me.

"Nur-rse?"

"I'm coming," I said busily. "I'll be back."

I was carrying a bedpan to the little bedpan hopper that was located at the corner of the ward where bedpans were cleaned and stored. My mate had gone on her break and no one else was around.

The voice called again, insistently this time. "Nur-rse?"

"I'm coming, I'm coming! Hold on! I'm just going to the hopper."

I stepped around the corner. This time the same voice was right at the back of my neck.

"NUR-RSE!!"

Slowly I turned around. There was nobody there! My hair stood on end. What to do? I had to decide in a flash. Drop the bedpan and run up the little ramp leading to the second wing? Continue on my way?

I opted for the second choice. In retrospect, it was a good thing I didn't drop the bedpan -- it would have made such a mess! I put the pan in the hopper and went back to the ward but I can tell you this, I was ice cold and shaking like a leaf.

It's one of those things, you know.

FOOTPRINTS

I'm a Registered Nurse. A health care aide and I were providing care in a private home for an extremely ill, bed-ridden gentleman who was both belligerent and nasty. I had been preaching to him that he had better say he was sorry to a few people, even though he wasn't particularly religious.

The beautiful white carpet in his affluent bedroom was spotless as this particular evening the health care aide had vacuumed it in her usual fastidious fashion. She liked to know exactly where she had already vacuumed. She did it perfectly and she did it once, always vacuuming in one direction. This way there were none of the usual ridges of smooth, rough, smooth, rough. That was her thing.

Fifteen minutes after she finished vacuuming, she went in to check on our patient. She found that the room was icy cold, absolutely freezing. As she looked around, she saw footprints on the carpet leading from the dressing table to the bed, where they disappeared.

I was preparing the medications when she bounded into the kitchen and said, "Let me see your shoes!"